DINOSAURS
AND THE BIBLE

D1456674

BRIAN THOMAS

HARVEST HOUSE PUBLISHERS
EUGENE, OREGON

All Scripture quotations are taken from the New King James Version®. Copyright © 1982 by Thomas Nelson, Inc. Used by permission. All rights reserved.

Cover by Institute for Creation Research

Cover photo © Catmando / Fotolia

DINOSAURS AND THE BIBLE
Copyright © 2013 Institute for Creation Research
Published by Harvest House Publishers
Eugene, Oregon 97402
www.harvesthousepublishers.com

ISBN 978-0-7369-6540-8 (pbk.)
ISBN 978-0-7369-6541-5 (eBook)

All rights reserved. No part of this publication may be reproduced, stored in a retrieval system, or transmitted in any form or by any means—electronic, mechanical, digital, photocopy, recording, or any other—except for brief quotations in printed reviews, without the prior permission of the publisher.

Printed in the United States of America

16 17 18 19 20 21 22 23 / VP / 10 9 8 7 6

ACKNOWLEDGMENTS

I owe a host of generous people lifelong debts of gratitude. Without them, this booklet would have either never been written or would have emerged a mediocre mess. Chief among the many are these: foremost, my mother, Jane Thomas, who taught me how to write a research paper in the sixth grade. I have not stopped writing since. The late Dr. Henry Morris's books on scientific evidences convinced me that molecules-to-man evolution was wrong and the Bible is right. Dr. Bill Cooper acknowledged me in a few of his books, all of which are indispensable and available in digital formats, and I am more than happy to return the gesture. Also, Beth Mull's endurance through editing something like 1,000 of my articles for the Institute for Creation Research has made me a much better writer over the last five years. Finally, I thank Dr. John Morris for general encouragement and for reviewing this manuscript.

CONTENTS

INTRODUCTION

When I first saw a dinosaur fossil as a small child, I was shocked by the enormous, tooth-filled skull that greeted me at the museum entrance. But very soon I was hooked. As the terror subsided, basic questions filled my mind. Where did dinosaurs come from? Where did they go? How long ago did they live? How did the Earth preserve their skeletons?

Over the years, teachers, museum guides, books, magazines, movies, and TV news reports provided the same general answers. Where did dinosaurs come from? I was told that they evolved long ago and lived on Earth for millions of years. Where did they go? Something happened 65 million years ago that wiped them out—perhaps mammals ate all their eggs, or maybe it was a violent impact from outer space. Supposedly, their bodies were fossilized over eons as minerals replaced the original bone material. For a long time, I saw no reason to doubt these answers.

That all changed with one conversation.

When I was a science major in college, a nonscience friend asked me a question I had never heard before: Is it true that a dinosaur fossil is dated by the age assignment given to the rock layer it's found in, but that this same rock layer is dated according to the million-year age assignments of the unique fossils it contains? Had I encountered this use of circular reasoning in my science studies? Could I show that dinosaur age assignments rest more on field data and less on assumptions or fallacies?

For months, I had no desire to tackle the issue. In retrospect, I probably dreaded questioning one of my own fundamental beliefs. At the time, I did not understand that my answers to questions about dinosaurs reflected my beliefs about the history of the world in general.

I dodged my friend's repeated challenge until we finally brokered a deal. He would stop bothering me if I would read his book on creation. It presented information that first challenged and then eroded my faith in evolution and its long ages. In studying creation materials, I found real evidence that the Bible, not the words of fallible humans, conveys truthful world history. My hope is that this book may have a similar impact on its readers as they see the evidence that God's Word is accurate and true in all things.

Where did dinosaurs come from and how long ago did they live? My answers to these questions have totally changed. Maybe yours will, too.

1

WHEN AND WHERE DINOSAURS LIVED

Dinosaurs once roamed the earth in an amazing variety of shapes and sizes. We know from their fossil remains that a few of them were huge, the largest land creatures that ever lived. Some of them were undoubtedly terrible and monstrous. We also know that many dinosaurs were only the size of a turkey when full-grown.

Almost no one these days can escape being told that dinosaurs lived in an Age of Reptiles that ended 65 million years ago. These teachings, repeated now for generations, have no real merit; they are bereft of science or history to substantiate them. One purpose of this booklet is to open a window on the evidence found in abundant scientific and historical sources of dinosaur data. We will see that the details fit well with a straightforward reading of Scripture.

The Creation of Dinosaurs

According to Genesis, God created man and animals, plants to sustain their bodies, the Earth for them to live upon, and the universe as their setting. He did this in the span of six days. For Him to have created all things in just the way Genesis 1 describes would have been no problem for an all-knowing, all-powerful, personal God.

Did God directly create dinosaurs? Adding information from the New Testament to what is recorded in Genesis, it is evident that each member of the Trinity was involved in the creation of the universe and its inhabitants.[1] We infer that the Father conceived of the creation, the Son spoke the Father's will in the form of "let there be" commands, and the Spirit powerfully effected those commands. If this is true, then it follows that God the Father invented each dinosaur kind, Jesus commanded each to materialize, and the Spirit energized those commands to make dinosaurs real in body and soul.[2]

Through these means, God created the creatures that today we call dinosaurs on the final day of His creative activity. He made plants on Day Three, stars on Day Four, then air and sea creatures on Day Five. It was on Day Six that God made the creatures that live on land, whether creeping or walking, large or small.

What exactly was a dinosaur? First, they were reptiles. Unfortunately, unlike birds, which all have feathers, and mammals, which all have hair,[3] reptiles have no single trait that is totally unique by which we can easily identify them. We can say that they have scaly skin, but so do bird feet. We can say they lay eggs, but some do not, and birds as well as some mammals also lay eggs. So the best we can do is rule out other classes of vertebrates to discern whether a creature is reptilian.

Dinosaurs did have scaly skin. Their scales were not like fish scales, which are like tiny plates that grow out of and can be scraped off the skin. Reptile scales are thickened folds or bumps of skin. Some fossils preserve the impression of dinosaur skin and show detailed rosette patterns that the scaly skin displayed.

Some dinosaurs laid eggs. Maybe they all did, but we don't know for sure, since it is difficult to link a fossil dinosaur egg to the species that laid

George Sternberg discovered a duck-billed dinosaur mummy in 1908 in Montana's Hell Creek Formation. In 1912 Henry Osborn photographed and described its skin, which clearly shows scales, or thickened bumps of skin, just like that which appears on many living reptiles.

it. Dinosaurs had other reptile-like features, such as certain holes in their skulls. Taken together, the fossil evidence clearly places dinosaurs among the many different forms that fall under the reptilian category. But dinosaurs had an important difference from modern reptiles.

The legs of modern reptiles—like turtles, lizards, and alligators—stick out from the body, then angle down to the ground. Their feet are seldom situated directly below their bodies, but instead are placed out to the side. In contrast, dinosaur reptiles had legs oriented nearly straight to the ground from the hips. The two-legged dinosaurs would have walked somewhat upright, more like humans. Our legs also extend straight down from hips to the ground. The two-legged dinosaurs called theropods are thought to have been meat-eaters and had hips that in some ways resemble those of modern lizards. *Tyrannosaurus rex* was a theropod. Other two-legged dinosaurs called ornithopods had bird-like hip structures and often ate plants. Duck-billed dinosaurs called hadrosaurs were ornithopods. Even the four-legged dinosaurs' legs descended from the body directly to the ground.

Dinosaurs walked on land and were therefore created on Day Six. The key verse on this point is Genesis 1:25: "And God made the beast of the earth according to its kind, cattle according to its kind, and everything that creeps on the earth according to its kind. And God saw that it was good." Dinosaurs certainly qualified as "beast[s] of the earth."

The passage also says that God made each animal "according to its kind," which means that the very first animals were created in discrete forms. And because the Lord brought representative animal "kinds" to Noah (Genesis 6:19-20), and not just two animals that might have evolved into all other creatures, we can infer that the different kinds did not and do not interbreed. Living animals show the same fidelity to their kinds that we expect based on these words in Genesis. For example, cats always breed cats, whether tiger, mountain lion, or tigon varieties, and horses always breed horses, whether Clydesdale, mule, zebra, or zorse varieties.

It is important to note also in Genesis 1:25 that God made all the animals "good." When Adam named the animals (Genesis 2:19), he evidently named the dinosaurs, too. When he examined the *Deinonychus* dinosaur kind, with its terrible teeth and talons, would Adam have agreed that such a creature was "good"? Why not? Animals such as bears use their teeth and claws to eat berries and roots. Sharp teeth and claws are not inherently evil or necessarily designed for any originally evil purpose. But a creature with malicious behavior could use them to harm other animals or even humans. That's when teeth become fearsome.

Before sin entered the world, there was no death or predatory behaviors. Back then, dinosaurs were indeed good. According to Genesis 1:30, God provided plant material for all the animals to eat. Thus, in the beginning, dinosaurs that had large, sharp teeth used them to eat plants.[4] Maybe they enjoyed eating gigantic fruits that are today extinct. Other interesting reptiles lived among dinosaurs, as is known from their fossilized bones found mixed together in the same sedimentary rock layers. God must have made all of these during the creation week. Sometime since then, these creatures went extinct, as far as is known.

Other Extinct Reptiles

God created flying creatures on Day Five, including flying reptiles. The Hebrew word often translated into the English word "birds" included more than just birds. God created the flying mammals, which are mostly bats, on Day Five as well. Like bats, flying reptiles possessed thin skin membranes stretched between elongated finger-like bones as wings. Their fossils are known as pterosaurs, but there is plenty of evidence throughout ancient history that people living near them called them various names, including "dragon." Fossils of pterosaurs and dinosaurs sometimes occur in the same rock layer, along with an array of very familiar sea creatures and swamp-dwelling animals and plants.

Interpretations of pterosaur fossils have changed over time. Many years ago, secular scientists suggested that pterosaurs probably could not fly. They thought that pterosaur anatomy was too clumsy for flight and conjectured that maybe they could only glide. But recent studies using both physical and computer models revealed that pterosaurs had all the necessary biological equipment to have been adept flyers. Scientists studying fossil tracks in southern France even worked out the ways that pterosaurs adroitly folded their wings and hopped onto their elbows when landing.[5] Pterosaurs had tiny pteroid bones, one at the front of each wing. When extended, the bone held aloft a small flap. Like a bird's alula feather, this was critical to maintaining flight at low airspeeds. Without it, pterosaurs would have crash-landed. God did not forget the tiniest design detail.

The discovery of fully functional flight features like the retractable pteroid bone and foldable wing construction must disappoint secularists, since they have been searching for fossils to place onto an imaginary evolutionary path toward pterosaur flight. However, biblical creationists, who believe the Bible means exactly what it says when it describes how God created each winged creature "according to its kind," expected to find fully equipped flyers in the fossils (Genesis 1:21).

In addition to birds, bats, and flying reptiles, God also created all the creatures of the sea on Day Five. Genesis 1:21 calls special attention to the *tanniym*. Though some translators chose to render this word as "whales," the term includes more than that. English Bible translators who did their work hundreds of years ago may have been familiar with then-living dragons, because they sometimes translated *tanniym* as "dragon," "sea monster," or "serpent." Whether flying or swimming, the words "serpent" and "dragon," like the word "reptile," apply to a broad range of creatures. We will investigate more such Bible words in chapter 3.

Large and small extinct marine reptiles are well-represented as fossils in certain sedimentary rock layers. One extinct marine reptile kind called mosasaur grew almost 50 feet long. Their fossils have been found on every continent, including Australia and Antarctica. Another large marine reptile known from fossils is the plesiosaur, which sometimes grew to more than 50 feet in length. Mosasaurs featured very long tails, while plesiosaurs featured very long necks. Perhaps no creatures were better qualified to be *tanniym* than these.

So far, we have seen clear scriptural implications that God created all the marine and flying reptiles on Day Five, and that He created all land reptiles, including dinosaurs, on Day Six. Fossils confirm this by showing that each creature kind, though it expressed some variations in body form, appears perfectly complete in the fossil record if it appears at all. Not one fossil exists as an *undisputed* evolutionary transition from one basic type to another. In other words, for every fossil that one evolutionary scientist suggests was evolving, another evolutionary scientist disagrees.[6] Observational science agrees with the assertion that God made completed creatures.

Dinosaurs in the Fall and the Flood

In the beginning, dinosaurs were all "very good" (Genesis 1:31). There was no violence, so none of them had killed any other creature. This state of goodness did not last long. Soon after creation, the first two humans rebelled and disobeyed God. This rebellion is what the Bible calls sin. Being holy, God meted out the wages of their sin. In Genesis 3, the Lord cursed the serpent, the woman, the ground, and Adam. At that moment, the process of dying began that the Lord had promised as the consequence for eating the fruit of the tree of the knowledge of good and evil, saying, "In the day that you eat of it you shall surely die" (Genesis 2:17). In His grace, the Lord prepared some "tunics of skin" for Adam and the woman, soon to be named Eve, showing that the first animal death was a sacrifice to cover the nakedness exposed by sin (Genesis 3:21).

Did animals begin killing other animals immediately after the Curse? The Bible doesn't say. But by the time a millennium and a half had passed, animal killings must have been common. The years leading up to the worldwide Flood judgment were no doubt fraught with animal violence. Genesis 6:11-12 says, "The earth also was corrupt before God, and the earth was filled with violence. So God looked upon the earth, and indeed it was corrupt; for all flesh had corrupted their way on the earth." "All flesh" included dinosaur flesh, meaning that by this time even dinosaurs had been corrupted.

The only remedy was their destruction. "God said to Noah, 'The end of all flesh has come before Me, for the earth is filled with violence through them; and behold, I will destroy them with the earth'" (Genesis 6:13). By this time, the land-dwelling bird, mammal, and reptile kinds had somehow been spoiled—morphed into monsters that, although they retained their essential created forms, became ruined castoffs from their well-behaved original ancestors.

But the Lord did bring some dinosaurs to Noah, presumably to a staging ground from which Noah and his family brought them into the Ark at just the right time. The text is clear and repetitive, at one point stating, "They and every beast after its kind, all cattle after their kind, every creeping thing that creeps on the earth after its kind, and every bird after its kind, every bird of every sort. And they went into the ark to Noah, two by two, of all flesh in which is the breath of life" (Genesis 7:14-15).

This means that dinosaurs were on Noah's Ark. This is a laughable suggestion to those who have not studied how feasible it really was, but the dinosaurs could readily have been accommodated on board. Following are basic answers to some common "dinosaurs on the Ark" questions.

Q How could Noah have squeezed the hundreds of different dinosaur species into the Ark along with all those other animals?

A Noah's family did not bring each "species," but two of each "kind." Paleontologists make careers out of inventing species names, but there were really only about 60 different basic dinosaur kinds. So 120 dinosaurs averaging the size of a sheep would have occupied a small corner of the vast vessel.

Q How could Noah have fit enough food on board to feed all those voracious dinosaurs for a whole year?

A Noah could have fed the dinosaurs Genesis 1 vegetarian diets. He may even have known which plant products they preferred before the Fall, since Noah's father, Lamech, could have talked with Adam about it. Also, reptiles are famous for fasting from food. Dinosaurs probably ate less than the mammals or birds on board.

Q How could Noah have handled and husbanded such terrible toothy tyrants?

A It wasn't until after the Flood that God endowed animals, including dinosaurs, with a fear of man (Genesis 9:2). Perhaps this made their management much easier during the Flood. If not, we can be sure that Noah's family was at least as clever as modern humans who have successfully corralled virtually every land creature at one time or another.

Q How would the large dinosaurs like Diplodocus have fit onto the Ark's decks?

A The largest dinosaur egg is about the size of a football, so even the big-bodied behemoths began small. God would most likely have selected sauropod juveniles to put on the Ark.

What happened to the dinosaurs not on the Ark? They drowned in the Flood or were suffocated by mud, along with the other land-dwelling, air-breathing creatures. During that year, successive super-tsunamis sent sandy slurries sliding across land surfaces, swallowing everything in their paths. This, not impacts from outer space, is the origin of the vast majority of dinosaur extinction recorded in the fossil record.

The next chapter provides fossil clues that clearly fit the Bible's account of a worldwide catastrophic dinosaur demise by fast-flowing, water-borne sediment. Some fossil clues even suggest that dinosaurs were among the last land creatures to survive outside the Ark. Meanwhile, it must have been a miserable year for those on board the Ark. But they survived the ordeal, and after the Earth began greening again, Noah and his family eventually released the animals, including dinosaurs and pterosaurs, into the new post-Flood world. What happened to the creatures after that?

Dinosaurs Through the Ice Age

Because God commanded His creatures to multiply and fill the earth, He must have created them with the necessary abilities to do so. Animals immediately and instinctively began this task after the Flood. When animals are presented with a new environment, they typically colonize it. For example, the 1980 Mount St. Helens volcano eruption ejected steam and mud blasts that devastated thousands of acres in Washington state. Evolutionary ecologists predicted the flora and fauna would need a century to recover. But after only 30 years the entire area was already richly filled with animals and trees. Younger visitors have to be told that the disaster happened fairly recently because growth covers much of the evidence. Elk quickly spread tree seeds through their droppings. When young forests regrew, opportunistic animals entered and rapidly multiplied. After their rapid population growth, animals' birth rates fell to sustainable numbers.

Similarly, the whole Earth was barren and desolate immediately after the Flood. But powerful plant and animal colonizers quickly transformed it into a habitable land surface. Of course, creatures need water to successfully and rapidly fill new environments. Abundant evidence from both science and Scripture shows that the Earth experienced an Ice Age soon after the Flood, and that meant abundant water along Earth's equatorial latitudes.

Terrible Ice Age storms dropped plenty of rain. Archaeologists recognize the signs showing that the Middle East, which is now largely desert, was once tropical.[7] For example, although the great Sphinx monument in Egypt suffered most of its damage from rainwater erosion, it rarely rains in that land today. Satellite images even reveal ancient waterways buried beneath sand dunes in the Sahara.[8] Ruined cities throughout the Middle East show that people thrived there when the land was more lush and productive.

Abraham lived near the end of the Ice Age, although this "age" ended gradually, not abruptly. Abraham and Lot looked out over the Jordan Valley that today holds the Dead Sea, and Lot noticed that it was "well watered everywhere" (Genesis 13:10). Today it is dry except where purposefully irrigated, and its sparse flora no longer resembles the Garden of God to which Lot compared it.

In lands farther away from the equator, regularly occurring post-Flood supersize snowstorms built sheets of ice several thousands of feet thick. These covered continent-size regions in northern latitudes. In later years, the ice melted and eventually carved new valleys and left behind piles of characteristic rocky debris and colossal scrape marks. All that melting ice made its way to the ocean, which is today about 350 feet higher than it was during the peak of the Ice Age. If we could turn back the clock, the lower sea levels would reveal much more habitable land areas, including land bridges connecting continents. Dinosaurs could have travelled to distant lands across ancient bridges that today lie submerged.

The first post-Flood dinosaurs found agreeable habitats in the then-lush and tropical Middle East. They soon migrated, perhaps from one water hole to another, some moving into Europe and others eastward to China. Ample evidence from petroglyphs and widespread legends confirms that dinosaurs migrated to the Americas.[9] Native languages use an array of specific names for various land or water monsters the speakers' forebears must have encountered.[10] As ice retreated over the centuries, new habitats became available for the occasional dinosaur to colonize, along with many other creatures like wooly rhinoceros, pigs, deer, and large cats. The Bible records many droughts in the Holy Land and nearby countries. These probably represent the retreat of a lush Middle East climate. When that land dried, so did the dinosaur habitats.

The few dinosaurs that remained there were often hunted, as many dragon legends portray. St. George was reputed to have slain a dragon in the Middle East in the late AD 200s, and another legend holds that the prophet Daniel killed a dragon near Babylon centuries earlier. These two examples represent scores of historical accounts from around the world.

Some dinosaurs may have persisted long after the Ice Age. Chinese histories feature dragons alongside other real animals in the Chinese zodiac. Dragon legends, paintings, carvings, and even historical records abound in Europe. Several European place names still reflect the name of the dinosaur or pterosaur that once lived there, like Grindelwald in Switzerland, Worms and Drachenfels in Germany, Llyn-yr-Afanc (Afanc's pool) in Wales, and the Knucker Hole in England.

Historian Bill Cooper analyzed several ancient written accounts of dragon encounters. One, from England, was written in 1405:

> Close to the town of Bures, near Sudbury, there has lately appeared, to the great hurt of the countryside, a dragon, vast in body, with a crested head, teeth like a saw, and a tail extending to an enormous length. Having slaughtered the shepherd of a flock, it devoured many sheep. In order to destroy him, all the country people around were summoned. But when the dragon saw that he was again to be assailed with arrows, he fled into a marsh or mere and there hid himself among the long reeds, and was no more seen.[11]

Dinosaur Extinction

If dinosaurs were really on the Ark and lived after the Flood, then why do they no longer exist? It was probably not an impact from outer space that killed the dinosaurs, as secularists conjecture. Like other animals, "dragons" of various forms began filling the earth immediately after the Flood, but people did not follow them at first. Instead of obeying God's command to Noah and his family to multiply and fill the earth (Genesis 9:1), Noah's great-grandchildren assembled themselves into the first recorded post-Flood city, Babel. So, while mankind was staying together, dinosaurs were pioneering afield, unimpeded by people.

But after God intervened by imposing different languages (Genesis 11:1-9), families began spreading across the earth. The two main reasons why animals go extinct today should likewise apply to dinosaur extinction—loss of habitat and human hunting. When humans settle an area, they remove the threats to their children's safety. They both hunt the threatening animals directly and displace them by moving their fields and settlements into the animals' habitats. Pioneering natives had hunted the giant moa bird to extinction on the islands of New Zealand by about AD 1500. Newspapers around the world announced in 2011 that a poacher killed the last Javan rhino living in Vietnam. Dinosaur extinction continued long after the Ice Age, as climate changes from rising seas, melting snows, and droughts likely contributed to the loss of suitable habitats.

For many centuries after the Flood, people encountered dragons all over the world. That must be how dragon legends arose in so many places. The last European dragons evidently died in the late Middle Ages. Dragons went extinct in China sometime after Marco Polo visited, since he recorded his medieval encounters with them. There are some eyewitness reports of dinosaurs still alive in extremely remote tropical swamps in the Congo and Indonesian Islands, but these await more research. Discovering a live dinosaur or pterosaur in some isolated place would not surprise someone who believes in biblical creation, but it would present a daunting challenge for evolutionists to explain how it could have survived when its relatives went extinct "65 million years ago."

Notes

1. One such reference in the New Testament is Colossians 1:13-16: "He has delivered us from the power of darkness and conveyed us into the kingdom of the Son of His love, in whom we have redemption through His blood, the forgiveness of sins. He is the image of the invisible God, the firstborn over all creation. For by Him all things were created that are in heaven and that are on earth, visible and invisible, whether thrones or dominions or principalities or powers. All things were created through Him and for Him."

2. Dinosaur skulls show that they had nostrils, so according to Genesis 7:22, they had "soulish" life, translated as "the breath of the spirit of life."

3. Even dolphins have whiskers, which are lost soon after birth.

4. Since plants do not have the breath of life, when dinosaurs ate plant material death did not occur, but only a God-designed cycling of nutrients. For more information, see Morris, J. 1991. Are Plants Alive? *Acts & Facts*. 20 (9).

5. Thomas, B. Pterosaur Tracks Show Traces of the Great Flood. *Creation Science Update*. Posted on icr.org September 22, 2009, accessed February 4, 2013.

6. Scores of these disputed fossils are helpfully compiled and fully documented in an appendix in Morris, J. and F. Sherwin. 2009. *The Fossil Record*. Dallas, TX: Institute for Creation Research.

7. Vardiman, L. 2011. A Well-Watered Land. *Acts & Facts*. 40 (6): 12-15.

8. Thomas, B. Genesis and a Wet Sahara. *Creation Science Update*. Posted on icr.org November 3, 2008, accessed February 14, 2013.

9. Nelson, V. 2012. *Dire Dragons*, 2nd ed. Red Deer, AB, Canada: Untold Secrets of Planet Earth Publishing Company, Inc.

10. Thomas, B. 2010. Oblivious to the obvious: dragons lived with American Indians. *Journal of Creation*. 24 (1): 32-34.

11. Cooper, B. 1994. *After the Flood*. Chichester, UK: New Wine Press, 133.

2

DINOSAUR FOSSILS

Is there any reliable evidence from outside the Bible that might refute or confirm scriptural history? Most Westerners are thoroughly convinced that dinosaur fossils not only challenge but virtually disprove the historical accuracy of Scripture. As discussed in the first chapter, most people believe that dinosaurs lived for millions of years during an Age of Reptiles that ended 65 million or so years ago. Since this evolutionary concept contradicts a plain understanding of the Bible, they reason that the secular scientists are right and the Bible got it wrong.

But what does the evidence show? Let's examine the key features of dinosaur fossils to see whether the best interpretations of them most easily support biblical history or the secularist's evolutionary history. Before we do, though, we should first consider what science can and can't tell us about past events.

How to Examine Evidence

When scientists want to figure something out, they first construct a model of what they think is going on. That model is based at least partly on their belief system or worldview, which influences how they decide what the evidence means. Questions about origins involve more than laboratory science because they are about events and circumstances that can't be directly tested without a time machine. And the answers to those questions will be strongly influenced by a person's view of history.

Two examples of this kind of historical question are "Who committed this crime and when was it done?" and "How did dinosaurs originate and when did they die?" One should use the best methods of analyzing history to answer these. Examining evidence alone, like fossils or fingerprints, is probably not the best method because evidence does not speak for itself. Rather, we interpret evidence according to our worldviews.

From within the context of a particular worldview, though, we *can* discern which historical model best matches the evidence. To do this, we select the model that requires the fewest clarifications or rationalizations. Good historians consider all available evidence in the context of the various historical models into which that evidence could fit. The simplest story line that explains the most data is preferred.

However, the evidence alone does not necessarily lead those with differing worldviews to the same conclusion. This is because one's worldview helps determine which models and evidences are considered in the first place. Fossil evidence can fit into different historical models according to different worldviews.

For example, imagine finding a group of dinosaur fossils encased in a sedimentary rock formation. Did a local flood cause a stream to violently overflow its banks and produce a rock layer filled with fossils, or could the mud, sand, and creatures have been deposited in that particular spot during one phase of a worldwide flood? An objective historian should consider either model as the possible explanation. For better or worse, though, we usually restrict our own thinking to models that fit the basic beliefs that define our worldviews.

Not all evidences carry the same importance. Circumstantial evidence, like fingerprints and fossils, can be interpreted by a wide range of models within differing worldviews. That is why good lawyers understand that the best evidence comes directly from those who experienced and recorded the events in question. Because Genesis provides this in the form of reliable eyewitness accounts, we confidently used it in chapter 1 to interpret dinosaur data.

Let's see if a biblical worldview that includes biblical history can frame dinosaur fossil evidence with fewer clarifications and rationalizations than competing historical models such as evolution.

Fossil Graveyards

Dinosaur fossils most often occur as mineralized bone fragments within a single sedimentary rock layer, sometimes only three or so feet thick, sandwiched between layers that have very few fossils. One such "bone yard" discovered in Canada covers a square mile and is loaded with what must have been an enormous *Centrosaurus* herd.[1] But this is by no means the largest such graveyard. Some bone beds extend for dozens of miles. Many of them lie in the western United States, but most continents contain such beds. What kind of processes could have made these?

Secular scientists imagine and reimagine historical models to explain dinosaur fossil graveyards. Almost all of these explanations call upon small-scale or slow processes occurring at similar rates and intensities as today's processes, like local floods or slowly transgressing seas. But each of these stories requires rationalizations to explain the difficulties they add. For example, if dinosaurs were overwhelmed and buried by local floods, then why do such floods never fossilize large (or even small) creatures when they occur today? Plus, local floods deposit their loads in thick clumps, often within a river channel. Something very different was required to spread the dinosaur

Dinosaur fossils are most often found in bone beds, mixed with the bones of other reptiles, mammals, and birds. Image: Institute for Creation Research

body parts into a thin, flat mud layer sometimes stretching across several states, and then cover them with another mud layer before the first layer hardened. Whatever really caused fossil graveyards needs to also explain how the dinosaur carcasses avoided rotting before they could be fossilized.

Most non-Christian evolutionists are unconcerned with the Bible's history of the Earth and outright ignore the Genesis Flood as a possible explanation for the evidence. But Christian anti-Flood geologists, who often teach in Christian universities, seek to reconcile the history that Scripture provides with the evolutionary history on which their main-stream colleagues insist. How do they make it work? By pretending that the Flood narrative is a myth and then dismissing it. They claim that a global flood would have been too chaotic to produce any sedimentary layers, let alone layers that contain dinosaur remains. But this claim ignores experiments showing that fast-flowing dirty water can deposit layers.[2] It ignores the evidence from Mount St. Helens's volcanic eruptions that laid down mud into layers while it was flowing at 100 miles per hour. It also ignores careful Bible study by oversimplifying complicated Flood processes.

Those who aren't very familiar with the Genesis Flood account think of it as a period of 40 days and nights of rain, but Scripture says the Flood lasted for a year, which would have involved lots of water and mud. Successive tsunami-like waves must have surged farther and farther inland for months until the water covered Earth's entire surface. During its peak height, the water would have washed to and fro from lunar tides, tectonic upheavals, and other complicated effects. In fact, Genesis 8:3 uses a Hebrew phrase, *halôkh vashûbh*, translated into the single English word "continually," to say just that.[3] As the floodwaters were draining, they were "going and returning again."

What better historical model to explain a dinosaur fossil graveyard than one of these Flood tsunami "mega-washings"? It provides the un-imaginably high energy of fast-flowing muddy water that could have knocked these huge reptiles off their feet and scattered their remains. Perhaps as the water reversed direction, it dismembered its load of plants, dinosaurs, and other animals, and sorted the larger body bones from smaller ones. Washing them far away from their original location, the waters buried the remains within vast and flat sedimentary graveyards. This would also mean that the dinosaurs in lower layers did not live in some earlier epoch, as evolutionists believe. They were just in an area that the Flood inundated earlier than the creatures whose carcasses were washed into upper layers.

The Flood explanation appears to require a few rationalizations of its own, and we will address an important one when we consider dinosaur footprints below. But the Flood account as told by Noah's sons Shem, Ham, and Japheth[4] totally trumps the competition in explaining the most significant and obvious aspect of dinosaur fossils—the fossil graveyards.

Going on a Dinosaur Dig

How do paleontologists go about unearthing the fossils they so diligently study? I found out in the summer of 2014, when Institute for Creation Research IT expert Daryl Robbins and I participated in a dinosaur dig near Glendive, Montana. Volunteers from the Glendive Dinosaur and Fossil Museum helped the effort on a stretch of private Badlands property, and for three days we worked with about a dozen other creation advocates, including Harry Nibourg, Vance Nelson, and Gary and Mary Parker.[5] During our adventure, we photographed and sometimes even handled rocks and fossils that confirmed the reality of Noah's Flood. As we drove home, Daryl and I discussed our time in the field, agreeing on which aspects of the experience we did and did not expect.

One thing we expected was the heat—well over ninety degrees each day. Even though we live in North Texas where summer temperatures soar into triple digits, we spend most of our time inside air-conditioned places. So, for the dig, we equipped ourselves with plenty of water.

We had hoped to discover dinosaur bones buried in rock layers, and the Lord blessed us with that and more. Daryl excavated a tail vertebra from a yet-unidentified dinosaur. To identify the dinosaur kind that matches his bone, Daryl will begin by comparing it to various ceratopsian backbones since we were digging in the Hell Creek Formation known to hold many *Triceratops* remains.

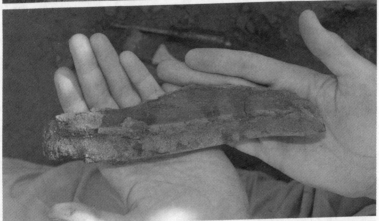

Top, workers including Dr. Gary Parker methodically scrape and brush away
sediment, revealing swamp and aquat-
ic plant and animal fossils long hidden
beneath the landscape near Glendive,
Montana. Above, author Brian Thomas holds a dinosaur bone fragment. The
dark patches are glue used to stabilize
fractures. Right, ICR's Daryl Robbins,
visible above wearing a cowboy hat,
points to the softshell turtle carapace
fragment he discovered and excavated.
Images: Brian Thomas (top two) and
Daryl Robbins

The same rock formation holds worldwide fame for dinosaur remains that contain original blood vessels and cells. For this reason, I am far more interested in discovering whether or not the dinosaur bone fragment I collected still holds dinosaur proteins than I am in identifying which dinosaur kind unwittingly donated its body part to my research. Experiments clearly demonstrate that even the most resilient original-bone tissue should not last a million years. If proteins are discovered in my bone, they would confirm what secular scientists have already described in their specimens from this same formation—that these fossils and rocks appear thousands, *not millions*, of years old.

Thinking about dinosaur-bone proteins reminds me of something that neither Daryl nor I expected. We came prepared to dig through hard, dry, rocky material. Instead, every time we speared the Hell Creek material with a screwdriver, sand sloughed off with relative ease. Years ago, I extracted an earthworm fossil from hard Texas limestone with exceeding difficulty. However, there in Montana fossils can be exposed with little more effort than it takes to dig a sand castle moat at the beach.

This ease was due to another surprising aspect of our dig, which was the wetness of the material surrounding our fossils—even six feet below the surface. Sagebrush grew above our digging and brushing area, sending its roots all the way down to the fossil-rich zone. The roots extract water from such depths, as well as vital nutrients supplied by decaying fossil bones and wood. How many millennia of plant root penetration would it take to completely remove all trace of these fossils from their damp sedimentary surroundings?

The museum officially owns all dig finds, but unless someone extracts a very remarkable fossil, the museum's kind managers let diggers keep their discoveries. So we placed our newfound fossils inside plastic bags. When exposed to sunlight, water immediately condensed inside the bags, showing that the fossils held some water. How on Earth could original tissues have lasted for 67 million years while damp?

Finally, the list of different kinds of fossils amazed us. Daryl carefully removed a large softshell turtle shell fragment. Another digger extracted a hardshell turtle leg bone. Here are some of the interesting fossil fragments the team found:

- Crocodile skull fragment
- Gar fish scale
- Shark tooth
- Redwood tree cone
- Horsetail rush stem segment
- Fig
- Seedpod

Of all the specimens we uncovered, only the dinosaurs have gone extinct. Why didn't tens of millions of years of evolution make any significant transformations to so many easily recognizable organisms? Daryl and I saw evidence of creation according to kinds, with no evolutionary advances or retreats (except for the unhelpful extinctions) in life forms. We also saw no evidence for deep time in these fragile fossils but rather evidence for recent widespread flooding. What a joy it was to dig dinosaur and other fossils with people who apply God's Word not only to their personal lives but also to the rocks—rocks that speak to us today.

Dinosaur Tracks

One of my favorite memories of camping is a long walk with my friends down the Paluxy River bed late one moonlit night. That year saw the most severe central Texas drought in most people's memories. There was so little water that the normally sizeable river stopped flowing. As a result, we were able to see scores of theropod, sauropod, and other large-dinosaur footprints usually hidden underwater. We wondered aloud if it was during, before, or after the Flood when those enormous reptiles stepped in the mud that would soon harden into the very limestone on which we were walking. One mystery lingered in my mind after that experience. If the Flood was responsible, then why were just the *dinosaurs'* tracks recorded? Why not those of the bears, cats, or emus that must also have been living at the same time as the pre-Flood dinosaurs?

Sometimes it takes a long time to discern which historical model incorporates the most data with the fewest rationalizations. Over the years, I sifted through the clues. The first clue was the largest—the Glen Rose Formation that includes the Paluxy River site extends from north Texas down toward the Gulf Coast and to parts beyond. No small, local flood could accomplish this. The broad, flat former mud plains suggested to many evolutionists that the dinosaurs and pterosaurs that left tracks walked across the shore of a vast and shallow inland sea. They imagined the sea slowly draining and refilling many times over millions of years to form the stack of repeated limestone and clay layers.

But this story failed to fit the second clue—almost everywhere that the Glen Rose Formation is exposed, its contact with upper and lower rock layers is so tight that you can't squeeze a penny between them. Seashores slant downward toward the water and show ever-changing ripples, dunes, and erosion ruts, but these limestone rocks are flat and even for countless miles. Plus, seafloor mud today retains no layers. Worms, clams, and other marine creatures obliterate layers in mere months when they churn and burrow.[6] So far, the Flood explains fossil footprints with fewer issues than competing concepts. But can the Flood solve the mystery of the tracks being almost purely dinosaurian?

Fossilized turtle, bird, crocodile, and armored dinosaur bones like those from *Ankylosaurus* are found with the bones of the dinosaur kinds that made the tracks. What would have kept them from stepping in the same places where the huge three-toed dinosaurs trod? Miners over the years have even noticed dinosaur footprints on top of coal layers, which resulted from vast plant-matter mats that were marooned on mud flats and later heated and compressed. But only the large theropod feet left tracks on the upper surfaces of certain coal seams, limestones, and sandstones. Why are there no baby *Triceratops* prints upon them, for example?

The Flood explains these tracks. During the weeks when the Flood's water was near its highest level worldwide, sea levels in the highest zones would have briefly dropped, exposing freshly deposited mud to the air. The baby dinosaurs and turtles, bears and emus had all died. Some were too small and floodwaters overwhelmed them. Others, like *Ankylosaurus*, were poor swimmers. Perhaps among the very last land creatures to breathe air outside the Ark were three-toed dinosaurs and a few sauropods. A single dinosaur walking exhausted under stressful conditions for five days and nights could stomp around enough to form 155,000 tracks.[7]

After dinosaur footprints were pressed into the mud, something was needed to seal them in place and preserve them. During this portion of

Over 100 theropod dinosaur tracks in a continuous left-right sequence adorn a hard limestone layer in the north Texas Paluxy River bed. Preservation required rapid covering and hardening. Image: Brian Thomas

the Flood, sediment-laden water washing again over the whole area would soon deposit yet another sedimentary layer—flowing slowly enough not to spoil the prints, and soon enough after the prints were made to protect them from erosion or churning by clams and worms.

I was fortunate to investigate what may be the longest continuous dinosaur trackway in the Western Hemisphere, a sequence of 135 *Acrocanthosaurus* tracks on the Paluxy River just upstream from Dinosaur Valley State Park. The dinosaur walked in a mostly straight line. Living creatures in natural habitats typically wander back and forth when foraging. Was the dinosaur that made these tracks under duress, and was it on its last legs as it wearily walked across a plain of briefly exposed mud near the height of Noah's Flood? Whereas the Flood offers a reasonable scenario for large-dinosaur fossil tracks, secularists still need to explain them.

Dinosaur Design

Some evolutionists claim that certain dinosaurs and other mostly extinct creatures in the fossil record appear to be incompletely or imperfectly formed. According to them, the supposedly not-quite-right dinosaur bones show that they had not yet evolved into more "advanced" forms.

For example, during the years when "Brontosaurus" was considered a valid dinosaur name, common opinion held that sauropods, the largest land creatures that ever lived, were too bulky for their own skeletons to have supported their body weight.[8] Back then, they reasoned that these giant, four-footed, supposedly inadequate dinosaurs required a watery habitat to buoy their body's bulk. This idea better fits an evolutionary history, where nature is thought to have invented creature features by blind trial and error. Ill-formed sauropod skeletons would therefore represent some of evolution's errors. This was thought to be evidence against the Bible, since any God who implemented insufficient designs does not match the identity of the biblical Creator who is totally perfect, all-wise, and all-powerful.

However, further investigation turned the defective-sauropod idea on its head, revealing the exacting standards of its bone design features.[9] Tendons and ligaments would have attached to its vertebrae, enabling sauropods to balance their whole bodies adroitly and suspend their long necks and tails in the air instead of clumsily dragging them. Diligent paleontologists were even able to work out the limits to sauropod mobility, finding that some giant dinosaurs could possibly have briefly raised themselves up on hind legs. All this new information makes a big difference. The story of substandard sauropod design turned out to be substandard itself. And this means that the Genesis history of God creating and pronouncing the great creatures on Day Six "good" (so that even their skeletons were good) better accommodates the data. But expert engineering in sauropod bone structure goes much deeper.

First, sauropod vertebrae were designed to be lightweight. They feature depressions, raised ridges, and hollow portions. Other dinosaurs' vertebrae were dense and solid. If sauropods had possessed the denser bone of smaller, short-necked dinosaur kinds, they could have starved to death with necks too heavy to lift to reach the trees that provided their food! Another weight-saving feature involved their very small heads. God even designed them to have tiny, weight-saving brains in their heads, supplemented by auxiliary brains atop their hips. This way, sauropods could keep their heads held high, perhaps all day and night, long enough to easily eat the tremendous quantity of plant matter that was likely required to sustain their sizeable proportions.

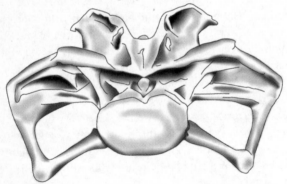

A single sauropod vertebra displays several weight-saving features that include internal hollows, weight-bearing structural ridges, and expertly placed cavities and indentations. Image: Susan Windsor

Sauropods' excellent and integrated skeletal design features are found from nose to toes! Sauropod hips were unique among all animals. The dinosaur's considerable body bulk balanced upon arches in its hips. Like ancient Roman arches that supported roofs, arched sauropod hips supported the animal's weight and transferred it down onto specialized pillar-like legs. Unlike other dinosaur legs, which bent at the knees most of the time, sauropod legs had a locking mechanism that kept them straight and stable to bear their body's burden.

God designed other dinosaurs with similar precision. So far, every claim by one evolutionist that a dinosaur fossil represents a transition between kinds has been counterclaimed by another evolutionist on the grounds of its well-formed anatomy. This ongoing disagreement stems from the fact that each dinosaur fossil appears to be from a fully formed creature with every part in place.

So we see that expert dinosaur design is a problem for evolutionary explanations. Evolutionists must invent extra substories to explain why there are no undisputed in-between dinosaur forms and why there are no good examples of evolution's design "blunders" among dinosaur fossils. On the other hand, expert dinosaur design follows directly from the Genesis creation account.

Variation in a Dinosaur Kind

It is clear from fossils that many dinosaur kinds expressed slightly different traits both within and between generations. For example, some are now convinced that *Dracorex hogwartsia*—whose many horns around its head made it look very much like depictions of European and Chinese dragons—lost its horns as it grew into the larger *Pachycephalosaurus*. Similarly, some suspect that smaller, many-horned ceratopsian dinosaur species lost horns and grew to become *Torosaurus*, which had two large holes near the back of its giant head frill. In these and similar cases, different dinosaur names might actually refer to different life stages of a single dinosaur kind.

But dinosaurs also expressed certain variations between generations. For example, scientists have discovered and named over 20 different ceratopsian dinosaur specimens that, though they show variations in body size, number of horns, and other skeletal differences, might all belong to one originally created ceratopsian kind. Of course, we cannot test this hypothesis without breeding studies, which are impossible to perform on

Amateur archaeologists discovered this dragon-headed dinosaur skull fossil, probably just a juvenile pachycephalosaur, in a portion of the Hell Creek Formation that extends into South Dakota. Image: The Children's Museum of Indianapolis

extinct creatures. But all ceratopsians shared certain anatomical features like short necks, four feet, and beak-like mouths.

Meanwhile, evolutionists diligently but fruitlessly search for any possible fossil that might represent some kind of evolutionary transition from any other dinosaur kind toward a ceratopsian. Contrary to their expectation, dinosaur fossils occur either as ceratopsian or not, with no undisputed in-between candidates. Thus, the idea of variation *within* a created kind fits these fossils much better than evolution's idea of changes *between* kinds. And with no changes between kinds, no one creature could ever develop into a totally different creature, as evolution requires.

Does the Bible allow variations within a dinosaur kind? Considering God's original purpose for animals, the answer should be yes. In Genesis 1, God blessed animals and humans specifically for them to be fruitful, multiply, and fill the earth. That is, they were to produce offspring and thus increase in number until they occupied all the habitable environments. God foreknew that Earth's environments would continually change. After all, a creature immediately alters the very environment that it comes to inhabit. Surely the Lord would have programmed His plants and animals to express trait differences that would facilitate each creature's ability to fit into those changing environments. It therefore comes as no surprise that dinosaurs present trait variations to their surroundings, either in a single generation or over several generations.

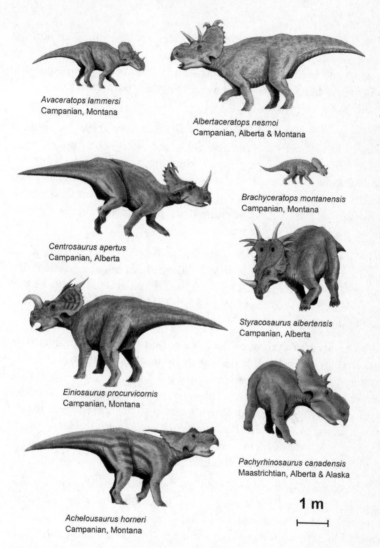

Avaceratops lammersi
Campanian, Montana

Albertaceratops nesmoi
Campanian, Alberta & Montana

Brachyceratops montanensis
Campanian, Montana

Centrosaurus apertus
Campanian, Alberta

Styracosaurus albertensis
Campanian, Alberta

Einiosaurus procurvicornis
Campanian, Montana

Pachyrhinosaurus canadensis
Maastrichtian, Alberta & Alaska

1 m

Achelousaurus horneri
Campanian, Montana

Although ceratopsian dinosaurs exhibited remarkable variations in their body sizes, bony frills, and number of horns, they remained faithful to a "ceratopsian" body plan—just as expected if they multiplied to fill Earth's environments and yet reproduced according to their own kind. Image: Nobu Tamura

Fossil "Feathers"

For decades nobody thought to suggest that dinosaur skin was adorned with anything but scales. But now most dinosaur books, museums, and even fossil professionals don't just say that some dinosaurs *might* have had feathers—they are certain that "feathered dinosaurs" actually walked the Earth.

Feathered dinosaurs have become all the rage for at least two reasons. First, a now-famous and increasingly large collection of dinosaur fossils from China features interesting-looking thin, straight fibers. Some evolutionists have suggested that these fibers represent transitional "protofeathers" as dinosaurs began evolving into birds. As we will shortly show, however, there is a more scientifically sound explanation for dinosaur fibers than that they were feathers.

So far, none of these fibers display any branching patterns like actual bird feathers have. They don't look like feathers, but they do look like something that more paleontologists should have recognized before they jumped so quickly to the very improbable feathered-dinosaur idea. Why would these scientists move ahead of the data?

The answer to this question is the second reason why "feathered dinosaurs" are in vogue. It is because the notion fits so well with the evolutionary story of some reptile having evolved into the first bird. Thus, it was natural for those who were already committed to evolution to readily misinterpret the discovery of these unique fossil fibers as feathers. In other words, a more bird-like dinosaur—such as one with feathers—would fill one of the many gaps in an imaginary dinosaur-to-bird lineage. So far, three observations clearly refute the feather interpretations.

First, many of the *fibered* dinosaur fossils lie in rock layers that also contain fully formed birds. Because they lived and died at the same time, they do not show any ancestor-descendant relationships. In addition, scientists found fossil bird tracks in sedimentary rocks containing the "oldest" dinosaurs (assuming for the sake of argument the evolutionary age assignments for rock strata).[10] The few evolutionists who are even willing to consider this bird track and bird fossil evidence rationalize it into their worldview. They claim that although *these* feathered dinosaurs from China were not evolving into birds, perhaps they look like the earlier dinosaurs (of which no fossils have yet been discovered) that *did* evolve into birds. But if the dinosaur fibers are simply not feathers, then we can avoid these mental gyrations.

The second observation that refutes the feather interpretation has to do with fossil skin. We know what bird skin looks like. People who pluck chickens know that each feather is rooted in a deep depression called a follicle. Also, researchers know what dinosaur skin looked like because they have examined skin impressions and even rare instances of original mummified dinosaur skin. It looked like today's scaly reptile skin. Its "scales" are actually thickened bumps of skin, hardened by keratin protein. Large bumps were spaced apart and surrounded by smaller bumps, often in rosette patterns. But no dinosaur skin fossils have yet shown even one follicle. If the fibers were feathers, then how did they attach to the thick, tough, scaly reptilian dinosaur skin?

The third observation that refutes dinosaur feathers is the most important. Scientists have tested animal skin degradation in water, protecting it from scavengers.[11] They witnessed the best explanation for dinosaur fossil fibers. After several days, rotting animal skin frayed at its edges. Microbes and chemicals first consumed the skin proteins that were easiest for them to digest, leaving behind tougher, stringy protein fibers. The fibrous skin components looked virtually identical to the Chinese fossil dinosaur fibers. So, not only do the dinosaur fossil fibers *not* look like feathers, they *do* look like partly decayed animal skin.

The dinosaur "feather" idea serves as an evolutionary icon, and the dinosaur fossil fibers have been trumpeted as proof. But because they are more likely just fibers from dinosaur skin that partly rotted in water, they should instead be seen as representing catastrophic flooding.

Original Tissue Fossils

When I saw my first dinosaur fossil as a child in a Wyoming natural history museum, I asked the museum attendant (with my mother's help) what this creature was and where its bones came from. The worker explained that these were not bones, but rocks in the shape of bones. She said that minerals had replaced all of the original bone material over millions of years.

Imagine my surprise, then, when I learned much later of the discovery of soft and pliable blood vessels still contained in a *Tyrannosaurus rex* femur bone. Blood vessels are not minerals. They are made of proteins that do not last millions of years. This was the first of many instances of original-tissue fossil discoveries that challenged the most basic tenets that I thought I knew about dinosaur fossils.

It appears that some dinosaur and other animal fossils are not pure rock, but are essentially mummified—dried remains surrounded by minerals and encased in rock. As expected, the mainstream scientists whose entire careers rest on evolutionary tenets did not at first believe the reports. Many of them still refuse to acknowledge even the possibility of original body tissues from dinosaurs, but their refusal to budge is not for lack of evidence. Original dinosaur tissues and specific biochemicals assuredly still lie underground in unique fossil pockets all over the world, awaiting discovery. Scores of technical reports published in all the mainstream science journals continue to reveal field evidence that utterly refutes those who dismiss the notion of original tissue fossils. We posted 40 or so such reports on the Institute for Creation Research website in 2011.[12] More have been published since.

By original tissue, we mean animal remains that were not mineralized. In other words, minerals did not replace all the tissue. We have seen mummified skin with scales, purple retinas, stomach and intestine lining, blood vessels, bone fibers, and ligaments. Secular scientists noticed whole cells within some of the tissue, including skin cells, bone cells called osteocytes, and red blood cells. More often, the remains have decayed so much that the only original substances left are tiny tissue fragments, such as proteins. As expected, the proteins are partly degraded, but they retain enough integrity for experts, using precise chemical procedures, to identify hemoglobin, elastin, osteocalcin, histone, ovalbumin, collagen, and others. These come only from animals with backbones, like dinosaurs.

The reason these original tissue discoveries are so stunning is because we know that such tissues have a shelf life, like food in a pantry. They react with other chemicals, spontaneously disorganize, and turn into dust over time. For instance, the range of experimentally determined rates at which collagen protein decays is well-known. A generous time-to-dust

Original Tissue Throughout the Fossil Record

QUATERNARY 2.6 my?	Wooly mammoth: Hundreds of partially decayed proteins
NEOGENE 23 my?	Salamander muscle: Whole and intact
PALEOCENE 65.6 my?	Penguin feathers: Pigments and pigment cells Lizard skin: Keratin protein and scales
CRETACEOUS 145.5 my?	Hadrosaur and *Tyrannosaurus* thigh bones: blood vessels and bone cells *Triceratops* horn core: soft sheet of flexible fibers
JURASSIC 201.6 my?	*Archaeopteryx*: faint feather protein signatures Squid: ink sac with dried ink
TRIASSIC 251 my?	Ichthyosaur: dried skin
PERMIAN 299 my?	Bacteria: still alive in deep salt deposit
CARBONIFEROUS 359 my?	Sea lilies: purple and yellow pigments
DEVONIAN 416 my?	Shrimp: red-colored shell
SILURIAN 444 my?	Scorpion: chitin and chitin-associated protein in exoskeleton
CAMBRIAN 488 my?	Sponge: chitinous skeleton fibers
EDIACARAN 630 my?	Beard worms: tubes with soft, flexible tissue

my = millions of years

© Institute for Creation Research

estimate of a dinosaur collagen specimen found in Montana is about 800,000 years (assuming the average annual temperature of the state of

Montana has been constant). You now see the conflict. Dinosaur fossils from Montana are said to be 68 million years old, but the collagen protein that their fossils contain restricts their age to 1/85th of that time.

In March 2013, I received carbon dates for Montana dinosaur bones. Since then, we have accumulated a couple dozen radiocarbon results from a variety of fossils, including seven different dinosaur species. I did not identify the bones as dinosaurian to the world-class U.S. laboratory that found plenty of radioactive carbon in them. All the carbon-14 in dinosaur bones should have long ago decayed into nitrogen if their evolutionary age assignments are real. Perhaps the reason why dinosaur bones still contain youthful radioactive carbon is because the bones—and the rock layers that contained them—are thousands, not millions, of years old. So, we have two "clocks" still ticking away inside dinosaur bones—protein decay and radioactive carbon decay. Both show that dinosaurs died off recently.

This evidence forces secular scientists to invent rationalizations. Some continue to deny that the decayed dinosaur flesh even exists, despite scores of detailed descriptions. Others deny that soft tissues decay as quickly as lab tests show they do, despite the repeatable data. Both parties could readily accept either scientific observation if they simply acknowledged that dinosaur fossils are only thousands of years old. But that idea does not fit with their worldview. As soon as a scientist admits to a young world, he or she would have to agree with the Bible that the Earth and its inhabitants came into being recently.

The Bible's history clearly lines up with the clues gleaned from fossils. Noah's Flood provides by far the most reasonable source of water and power required to deposit the massive fossil graveyards. The Flood also provides a solid historical setting for why only dinosaurs made the fossil tracks found in certain areas and how those layers (even including coal beds) often extend for miles without tilts or erosion ruts. Dinosaur fossils even show expert design, just as one would expect if God formed them on purpose. Finally, original dinosaur tissues, cells, and proteins fit Scripture's testimony of a world that is just thousands of years old. The most significant features of dinosaur fossils confirm creation and the Flood.

Notes

1. Thomas, B. Canadian "Mega" Dinosaur Bonebed Formed by Watery Catastrophe. *Creation Science Update*. Posted on icr.org July 13, 2010, accessed February 27, 2013.
2. For example, Julien, P. Y., Y. Lan, and G. Berthault. 1993. Experiments on stratification of heterogeneous sand mixtures. *Bulletin de la Société Géologique de France*. 164 (5): 649-660.
3. Morris, J. and J. J. S. Johnson. 2012. The Draining Floodwaters: Geologic Evidence Reflects the Genesis Text. *Acts & Facts*. 41 (1): 12-13.
4. Genesis 10:1 appears to be their signature on the preceding Flood account that began in Genesis 6:9.
5. Harry Nibourg built and owns Big Valley Creation Science Museum in Alberta, Canada. Vance Nelson is the director of Creation Truth Ministries in Alberta. Gary and Mary Parker are cofounders of the Creation Adventures Museum in Arcadia, Florida.
6. Morris, J. 2009. Sedimentary Structure Shows a Young Earth. *Acts & Facts*. 38 (7): 15.
7. Oard, M. J. 2011. *Dinosaur Challenges and Mysteries*. Atlanta, GA: Creation Book Publishers.
8. "Brontosaur" turned out to be the body of an *Apatosaurus* mismatched with a *Brachiosaurus*'s head.
9. Thomas, B. and F. Sherwin. 2011. What the Fossils Really Say about Sauropod Dinosaurs. *Acts & Facts*. 40 (11): 17-18.
10. Melchor, R. N. and S. de Valais. 2006. A review of Triassic tetrapod track assemblages from Argentina. *Palaeontology*. 49 (2): 355-379.
11. For example, Allison, P. A. 1988. The role of anoxia in the decay and mineralization of proteinaceous macro-fossils. *Paleobiology*. 14 (2): 139-154.
12. Fossil Analyses with Verified Original Soft Tissues. ICR Fact Sheet. Posted on icr.org/soft-tissue-list July 21, 2011, accessed February 4, 2013.

3

DINOSAURS IN THE BIBLE

So far, we have tried to show how Scripture best explains what fossils and human history reveal about dinosaurs. But additional insights from the Bible further establish the clear connection between dinosaurs and the Word of God.

What Was Behemoth?

When a Scottish friend recently visited my family's home in Texas, I asked how he was introduced to the Lord Jesus and how he came to believe in biblical creation. He told us that even though he grew up as a secularist, he responded to preaching about Christ during a church service that he visited in Spain. Only a few weeks later, a kind man from his new church asked him, "Did you know that dinosaurs were described in the pages of Scripture?"

He said he had no idea but was curious. So the man showed him Job 40. What a great way to introduce a new Christian to the trustworthiness of Scripture—showing how the Bible itself answers questions about dinosaurs!

In Job 40:15-24, God speaks to Job out of a whirlwind, inviting him to consider a very large creature and what its size and strength imply about God's greatness:

Look now at the behemoth, which I made along with you;

He eats grass like an ox. See now, his strength is in his hips, and his power is in his stomach muscles. He moves his tail like a cedar; the sinews of his thighs are tightly knit. His bones are like beams of bronze, his ribs like bars of iron. He is the first of the ways of God; only He who made him can bring near His sword. Surely the mountains yield food for him, and all the beasts of the field play there. He lies under the lotus trees, in a covert of reeds and marsh. The lotus trees cover him with their shade; the willows by the brook surround him. Indeed the river may rage, yet he is not disturbed; he is confident, though the Jordan gushes into his mouth, though he takes it in his eyes, or one pierces his nose with a snare.

Translators, unsure what modern animal might best represent behemoth, inserted English letters that sound out the original Hebrew. Occurring only here in Scripture, the word "behemoth" appears to be the masculine plural form of *behemah*. This term referred to many different animals in the Old Testament, typically those that walk on four feet, distinguishing them from flying animals. The King James Version translates the word as "cattle" in the early chapters of Genesis and as "beasts" in the Flood account. This could include sheep, bears, elephants, elk, alligators, and other quadrupeds. To which animal was God referring? Perhaps the best match for the Job 40 description is a sauropod.

First, we should determine why the category of *behemah* ("beasts") would include dinosaurs. Examining a comparable word in another language helps establish the definition of a word. The fact that multiple languages sometimes contain similar words indicates that the words carry a real and shared meaning. For example, the English word "dragon" refers to giant serpents—sometimes flying, but sometimes land-bound. Many languages share this similar-sounding word and they generally retain its meaning. *Draca* and *ddraig* in Anglo-Saxon and Welsh sound like the Polish word *drak*. Polish has its own word for dragon, *smok*, but may also have imported *drak* from other languages. *Drakon* is Greek, *draco* is Latin, and *dreq* is Albanian. Similarly, ancient languages shared the same-sounding word as *behemoth*, and it carried a similar meaning—

giant beast. The Egyptian word is *p'ihmw*, and the term in Arabic sounds much the same as in Hebrew.

Not only words, but artifacts can inform us. Conservative Bible scholars John Walvoord and Roy Zuck argue in *The Bible Knowledge Commentary* that behemoth was a hippopotamus, as do the translation notes in many English Bible versions. These authors state, "The hippopotamus was the largest of the animals known in the ancient Near East."[1] But how can they be sure of this if they weren't there? Actually, several artifacts appear to refute this assertion.

One in particular depicts two colossal creatures. Apparently, ancient Near Easterners were quite familiar with at least one creature that dwarfed the hippo. An exquisitely carved commemorative plaque called the Narmer Palette depicts a triumphant pharaoh on one side and symbols of greatness on the other. It looks as though the pharaoh in question wanted others to consider him more powerful than some of the most powerful creatures around—giant, four-footed, long-necked, long-tailed animals that should look familiar to those who read books about dinosaurs.

As we discussed earlier, the key anatomical feature that distinguished dinosaurs from other reptiles was that their legs pointed straight down from their bodies. And a key feature that distinguished sauropods from all other animals was their long necks. As you can see from the picture on page 46, the legs of the creatures on the Narmer Palette point straight down, just like those of sauropod dinosaurs that we know from fossils. Other animals like cats and dogs also walk on four downward-aimed legs, but no mammal has a serpentine-like neck such as that depicted on this and similar artifacts. If the artist carved the likenesses based on firsthand or secondhand reports, that would explain some of the differences between what we know about sauropod anatomy from fossils and the sauropod-like anatomy shown on the Narmer Palette. Other ancient depictions resemble even more closely the illustrations found in modern dinosaur books. Some of this pictorial evidence is featured in the book *Dire Dragons*.[2]

Could the name behemoth be a specific application of its root word (*behemah*, four-footed beasts) to dinosaurs that survived into and beyond

One side of the Narmer Palette, an ancient Egyptian plaque intended to glorify a pharaoh, depicts wranglers handling two giant, long-necked creatures that might reflect how Job's behemoth looked.

the Ice Age? With archaeology opening this possibility, we can further investigate the Job text.

Job may well have been looking directly at the creature while God was speaking since in Job 40:15 God told him to "look now at" it. In the same verse, God specified that He made behemoth "along with you." This means that He made both man and behemoth during the same time period. According to Genesis 1, He made all the beasts, including dinosaurs, and humans on Day Six.

Next, "he eats grass." Hippos eat grass most of the time, but some dinosaurs also ate grass. Scientists found microscopic bits of grass in fossil sauropod dung from India.[3] The discovery shocked secularists who had long taught that grasses evolved millions of years after dinosaurs had all gone extinct.[4] If they had taken their history from Scripture, which teaches that God made all the plants before He made dinosaurs, secularists would not have been so surprised.

The powerful "stomach muscles" of the behemoth clearly refer to the muscle-bound belly region. The *Apatosaurus* bone structure shows that its highest point was above its hind legs, upon which its body largely balanced. Surely, this or a similar dinosaur's midsection and thighs rooted its strength.

But the phrase "he moves his tail like a cedar" (v. 17) truly distinguishes behemoth from other animals. Commentators Walvoord and Zuck try to explain how this could refer to the tiny flap-like tail of a hippopotamus. They invoke the meaning "stiffens" from an Ugaritic word that sounds similar to the unique Hebrew verb for "moves." But if we replace "moves" with "stiffens," then we end up with an even better description of a sauropod tail, as scientists have learned within the last few decades. The fact that it stiffened implies that it could also go limp. Hippo tails are always "stiff." Unlike hippos, sauropod tails could be limp, stand out from the body when stiffened, or move like a giant tree trunk. Would anybody effectively use the analogy of either a "moving" or "stiffening" cedar tree to describe a hippo tail today?

Verse 19 says that behemoth "is the first [chief] of the ways of God," so it was evidently the largest land creature that God made. Today's hippos can reach three tons, but scientists estimate *Apatosaurus's* top weight exceeded 16 tons. It is therefore likely that even the post-Flood sauropods outweighed hippos. *The Henry Morris Study Bible* note for this verse says, "The behemoth was the 'chief' of all created land animals, which could only, therefore, have been one of the great land dinosaurs."[5]

What Was Leviathan?

The very next chapter in Job describes another mighty creature through which Job and his company could better know their Maker. This one was certainly a reptile, and certainly massive. Like behemoth, leviathan probably no longer exists. But unlike behemoth, which lived in marshes, this one swam in the sea (Job 41:31).

Leviathan's features identify it in general as an extinct marine reptile, but whether it was a long-necked plesiosaur, large-mouthed mosasaur, an enormous crocodile-like creature called *Sarcosuchus*, or any of the others known from fossils is not yet certain. We can rule out some possibilities—like birds, fish, and mammals—by following the Bible's clues. Leviathan's scale-packed hide (v. 15) was so tough that it repelled spears (v. 7). It was so large and powerful that it struck instant fear in the heart of any onlooker (v. 9). It had a nose (v. 2), so we know that it had to surface to breathe. Terrible teeth rimmed its mouth (v. 14).

Leviathan also had bright eyes (v. 18) and breathed fire from its mouth (v. 19), while its nostrils issued smoke (v. 20). To those of us who did not witness the creature, these features might sound hard to believe. But life forms can make fire and light. The lowly bombardier beetle defends itself with enzyme-activated steam blasts that issue from twin cannons mounted on the rear of its abdomen. Hundreds of very different creatures, including some vertebrates like sharks, generate light.[6] So, we know the Lord certainly possessed the engineering genius required to design and construct whatever biological structures leviathan needed to emit fire just like the text describes.

Although Bible scholars and translation notes suggest that leviathan was a crocodile, this interpretation doesn't align with the text. First, crocodiles do not breathe fire. Second, they do not strike the same level of terror into the hearts of onlookers as leviathan apparently did. Crocodiles live in swamps, rivers, and shores, whereas leviathan lived in the "deep"

(v. 31). According to Psalm 104:26, leviathan disrupted ancient shipping lanes. Even small oceangoing vessels would plow right over a crocodile.

In addition to references in Psalms and Isaiah, ancient extrabiblical records from around the world depict sea dragons that match the Job account better than a crocodile. The margins of very old maps feature giant marine reptiles right alongside recognizable sea life such as fish and lobsters. Why would people talented enough to create these high-quality and useful works lessen the integrity of their products by adding creatures from myth or fantasy?

Often, the old maps depicted their leviathans with a frill of soft tissue around the neck, like a collar that retracted or a folding Chinese fan. Job 41 does not mention this feature, but such a frill may well have been a part of the creature, since the word "leviathan" likely derives from two Hebrew words meaning "wreathed" and "dragon." The *Gesenius Lexicon* defines *leviathan* as "an (animal), wreathed, twisted in folds."[7] Did the ancient mapmakers base their drawings on information from people who witnessed enormous sea serpents that wore "wreaths" of foldable tissue around their necks? If so, they add their testimony to others and to Job that tremendous and terrible sea serpents recently roamed the world's waters.

What Was Nachash Saraph?

Numbers 21 relates a particular incident during the Israelites' decades-long wandering in the wilderness. When they spoke out against God, He sent "fiery serpents" (Hebrew *nachash saraph*) among them that killed many. God offered a way of salvation by instructing Moses to place a replica of the serpent on a pole. Any bitten person who looked at it would live. What were those serpents?

Most assume they were ordinary snakes, but that doesn't make sense of all the biblical data. If that were the case, couldn't the people have simply stepped out of the way? While descending a desert trail recently, my right foot came within an inch of a huge western diamondback rattlesnake. It is amazing how fast even an exhausted person can move when he suddenly encounters a venomous serpent. I imagine that the ancient Israelites were at least as agile as I am. This and other clues open the possibility that the animals in Numbers 21 were flying serpents.

Swedish historian and Catholic Archbishop Olaus Magnus created one of the earliest Nordic maps during the 1500s. It depicts an array of creatures still known today (like polar bears, reindeer, lobsters, and people), alongside large marine reptiles—possibly including *ketos* or leviathan.

Isaiah 14 and 30 mention such a creature, a being so unfamiliar to modern commentators that they suggest it is merely symbolic. Isaiah 14:29 says, "Do not rejoice, all you of Philistia, because the rod that struck you is broken; for out of the serpent's roots will come forth a viper, and its offspring will be a fiery flying serpent." What is a "fiery flying serpent"? Serpents don't fly, do they?

They may be extinct today, but flying serpents certainly lived in the past. Fossil flying reptiles are known as pterosaurs, a word meaning "winged lizard." Like the behemoth and leviathan, flying reptiles became extinct only recently, within human memory.[8] We are confident of this because, also like the behemoth and leviathan, flying reptiles have biblical roots and deep representation throughout recorded human history.

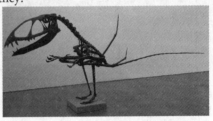

Dimorphodon was a long-tailed, large-headed pterosaur known from fossils. Did the ancients witness and record encounters with this or other flying reptiles? Image: David Peters

In Isaiah 14:29 and 30:6, the meaning of "fiery flying serpent" is clear. The Hebrew phrase includes a term derived from the verb *uph*, meaning to fly or flutter, moving back and forth like wings. The word *saraph* used in these verses can refer to fiery serpents, venomous serpents, shining serpents, flying dragons, and even certain angels. Isaiah distinguishes the fiery flying *saraph* from the angelic seraphs (seraphim) he saw standing near God's throne. The same word in Egyptian is *seref*, meaning "flying serpent."

Winged serpents are commonly depicted in Egyptian, Incan, and other cultures' artifacts.

Small seals from ancient Israel have flying serpents engraved on them. One example among many is a limestone seal discovered in the late 1970s. On the front "in classical Hebrew character, perfectly preserved, it reads: Belonging to Sadoq, son of Mikha." The back "is decorated with a two-winged *uraeus*," which is a serpent that is often featured in Egyptian and Phoenician art "and frequently found on ancient Hebrew seals."[9]

If paintings, carvings, and written descriptions carry meaning, then flying reptiles persisted through many centuries in many places around the world. They are shown in European castles, Native American pictographs, ancient books, weaponry, coins, and seals.

As another example, French naturalist Pierre Belon described a flying reptile in his 1553 book *Observations of several singularities and memorable things found in Greece, Asia, Judea, Egypt, Saudi Arabia and other foreign countries.*[10] In it, he drew pictures of people, plants, and animals he encountered while journeying to the Middle East, including a flying reptile. Belon discussed the dangerous serpent after his 30-day trip to a possible Mount Sinai location near Egypt and Arabia.

Belon's accounts convey sober and matter-of-fact details. Interestingly, his book includes a fine sketch of what is clearly an armadillo that he saw while visiting Turkey! Today, armadillos are restricted to North and

French naturalist Pierre Belon traveled to Middle Eastern and nearby countries, including modern Turkey, Israel, and Egypt, during 1546–1549, and described his journey's details in a 1553 book published in Paris. This sketch of a flying serpent is one of many sketches in his book of indigenous people, animals, and plants.

Today, armadillos only inhabit the Americas, but Belon encountered them in 16th-century Turkey.

Belon knew how to draw a regular snake, showing that he could distinguish between flying and crawling reptiles.

South America. If armadillos have gone extinct in Turkey within human memory, then why not flying reptiles from other regions?[11]

With the above observations in mind, let's consider the serpents in Numbers and Isaiah that are identified by the Hebrew phrase *nachash saraph*. Numbers 21:6 says, "So the LORD sent fiery serpents [the plural form of *nachash saraph*] among the people, and they bit the people; and many of the people of Israel died." Verse 8 says, "Then the LORD said to Moses, 'Make a fiery serpent [*saraph*], and set it on a pole; and it shall be that everyone who is bitten, when he looks at it, shall live.'"

If these were ordinary snakes, *nachash* would have been appropriate, or *akshub*, which means "adder" or "asp." It was not quite a flying dragon (*saraph*) and not merely a snake or general reptile (*nachash*), so it seems that it was a creature sharing bits of both aspects—a bright and flying snake-like reptile. More evidence from outside the Bible also indicates the presence of flying reptiles in perhaps the same desert regions near Egypt, and of Moses' possible familiarity with them.

For example, the Jewish historian Josephus, a contemporary of the apostles, recounted a legend of Moses in his book *Antiquities of the Jews*. Apparently, Egyptian royals selected Moses to lead their army against the Ethiopians, who had been successfully attacking Egypt. Moses had to overcome a fearsome obstacle.

> For when the ground was difficult to be passed over, because of the multitude of serpents, (which it produces in vast numbers, and, indeed, is singular in some of those productions, which other countries do not breed, and yet such as are worse than others in power and mischief, and an unusual fierceness of sight, some of which ascend out of the ground unseen, and also fly in the air, and so come upon men at unawares, and do them a mischief,) Moses invented a wonderful stratagem to preserve the army safe, and without hurt; for he made baskets, like unto arks, of sedge, and filled them with ibes [ibis birds], and carried them along with them; which animal is the greatest enemy to serpents imaginable, for they fly from them when they come near them; and as they fly they are caught and devoured by them, as if it were

done by the harts; but the ibes are tame creatures, and only enemies to the serpentine kind...As soon, therefore, as Moses was come to the land which was the breeder of these serpents, he let loose the ibes, and by their means repelled the serpentine kind, and used them for his assistants before the army came upon that ground.[12]

Can other ancient historians corroborate this batch of flying serpents in the Middle East? At least two, in fact. One very early account comes from Esarhaddon, king of Assyria, in 671 BC. Damaged text from an ancient tablet describes his army's march toward Egypt through the Sinai desert:

In accordance with the command of my lord Assur, my mind was set and my heart was pondering: I requested camels from all the kings of Arabia and had them carry water bags(?). I marched 30 double-hours (ca. 320 km) of ground, a journey of 15 days, through huge sand hills. I went 4 double-hours (ca. 43 km) of ground with alum stone...4 double-hours (ca. 43 km) of ground, a journey of 2 days. I trampled on two-headed serpents,...whose sight/touch/ breath meant death, and I marched on. 4 double-hours (ca. 43 km) of ground, a journey of [2 days, with] yellow [serpents] whose wings were batting(?). I marched 4 double-hours (ca. 43 km) of ground, a journey of 2 days,...15 double-hours (ca. 160 km) of ground, a journey of 8 days, ...Then the great lord Marduk came to my assistance...he kept my troops alive. 20 days...[13]

Apparently, the hazardous presence of serpents in this region persisted for many years, for in the mid-4th century BC, Greek historian Herodotus relates very similar information.

75. There is a region moreover in Arabia, situated nearly over against the city of Buto, to which place I came to inquire about the winged serpents: and when I came thither I saw bones of serpents and spines in quantity so great that it is impossible to make report of the number, and there were heaps of spines, some heaps large and others less large and

others smaller still than these, and these heaps were many in number. This region in which the spines are scattered upon the ground is of the nature of an entrance from a narrow mountain pass to a great plain, which plain adjoins the plain of Egypt; and the story goes that at the beginning of spring winged serpents from Arabia fly towards Egypt, and the birds called ibises meet them at the entrance to this country and do not suffer the serpents to go by but kill them. On account of this deed it is (say the Arabians) that the ibis has come to be greatly honoured by the Egyptians, and the Egyptians also agree that it is for this reason that they honour these birds.

76. The outward form of the ibis is this:—it is a deep black all over, and has legs like those of a crane and a very curved beak, and in size it is about equal to a rail: this is the appearance of the black kind which fight with the serpents, but of those which most crowd round men's feet (for there are two several kinds of ibises) the head is bare and also the whole of the throat, and it is white in feathering except the head and neck and the extremities of the wings and the rump (in all these parts of which I have spoken it is a deep black), while in legs and in the form of the head it resembles the other. As for the serpent its form is like that of the watersnake; and it has wings not feathered but most nearly resembling the wings of the bat. Let so much suffice as has been said now concerning sacred animals.[14]

One would have to work diligently to avoid the conclusion from archaeology, history, and Scripture that people encountered pterosaurs.

What Was Ketos?

Some type of Mediterranean Sea creature swallowed God's rebellious prophet Jonah when he tried to flee God's command to go to Nineveh. The sea creature carried Jonah for three days and nights before expelling him onto dry land to carry out his mission.[15] This creature is often described as a whale, but history identifies it as another creature entirely.

On display in the church at Fowlis Wester, Scotland, two wolf-headed sea creatures, likely *ketos*, were carved around 800 A.D. onto a large stone bearing a Celtic cross. Image: Lucien Tuinstra

Jonah's book uses a Hebrew word for the marine creature that is so general it could have included fish, whales, or marine reptiles—although whatever the creature was, Jonah identifies it as "great" in size. Matthew's gospel employs a more specific Greek word. Jesus said in Matthew 12:39-40:

> An evil and adulterous generation seeks after a sign, and no sign will be given to it except the sign of the prophet Jonah. For as Jonah was three days and three nights in the belly of the great fish ["whale" in the King James], so will the Son of Man be three days and three nights in the heart of the earth.

This was originally written in Greek, and the word that the King

James Version translates as "whale" was *ketos*. The problem is that Greek has other specific words that refer to whales, and *ketos* is not one of them.

Historian Bill Cooper recently helped answer this question in his remarkably relevant digital book *The Authenticity of the Book of Jonah*. Although knowing the animal's exact identity is not necessary to understand the plain meaning of the Matthew text, Cooper identified an array of sources from outside the Bible that accurately describe the *ketos*.

Ancients used *ketos* to refer to a marine reptile, now likely extinct. An ancient Greek version of the Old Testament likewise translated "great fish" from Jonah 1:17 with the phrase *ketei megalo*, meaning a huge *ketos*. In particular, it was a sea serpent with a dog-like head, apparently large enough to swallow a man whole. Bill Cooper noted the following 13 ancient authors whose writings shared this word and its serpentine definition:[16]

- Homer (9th–8th century BC)
- Euripides (ca. 480–406 BC)
- Aristophanes (448–380 BC)
- Lycophron (285–247 BC)
- Marcus Terentius Varro (116–27 BC)
- Diodorus Siculus (ca. 60 BC–AD 30)
- Manilius (1st century AD)
- Pausanias (2nd century AD)
- Claudius Aelianus in his *De Natura Animalium* (ca. AD 175–235)
- Oppian of Apamea (ca. AD 200)
- Eustathius (ca. AD 300–377)
- Hesychius (5th century AD)
- Johannes Moschus (6th century AD)

Early Christians in Rome and Europe painted, carved, and modeled *ketos* with consistent anatomy. For example, Cooper's book includes an image of a Roman painting of Jonah being thrown from a boat to a sea monster with a dog-like head. Various artifacts show a similar animal, such as third-century marble carvings from Turkey displayed in the Cleveland Museum of Art.

The famous 230-foot-long Bayeux Tapestry housed in Normandy, France, depicts William, Duke of Normandy, conquering England

Like other ancient ship prows, the one embroidered on the Bayeux Tapestry made during the 1070s and displayed in Bayeux, France, depicts a dog-like head and long neck—likely a sea serpent.

in 1066. One section depicts a dog-like head adorning a ship's prow. It looks similar to carved prows on some ancient Viking ships. And like their tradition of the thunderbird, Native Americans carry strong traditions—even totem pole carvings—of a serpentine "sea wolf." The church at Fowlis Wester in Scotland houses a Celtic cross carved around AD 800. At the top, it depicts what could be Jonah being swallowed by a *ketos*. A sign at the church states that the sea creature "with a wolf's head" swallows a man.

Together, these written, carved, and stitched eyewitness testimonies show that the Lord's earlier audience would have known exactly the kind of creature to which He referred—*ketos*, the dog-headed sea serpent.

Notes

1. Walvoord, J. F. and R. B. Zuck. 1985. *The Bible Knowledge Commentary: Old Testament.* Colorado Springs, CO: Victor Books, 772.

2. Nelson, V. 2011. *Dire Dragons*, 2nd ed. Red Deer, AB, Canada: Untold Secrets of Planet Earth Publishing Company, Inc.

3. "Some coprolites [fossil dinosaur dung] contain phytoliths, which are uniquely shaped microscopic crystals manufactured by various plant tissues. Most phytoliths are made of silicon dioxide, the same chemical that comprises sand. Scientists examining these tiny grains can often discern from which plant they came." Thomas, B. Dinosaurs Ate Rice. *Creation Science Update.* Posted on icr.org November 4, 2011, accessed March 8, 2013.

4. Sherwin, F. Dinosaurs, Grasses, and Darwinism. *Creation Science Update.* Posted on icr.org November 29, 2005, accessed March 8, 2013.

5. Morris, H. 2012. *The Henry Morris Study Bible.* Green Forest, AR: Master Books, 823.

6. Thomas, B. 2013. The Unpredictable Pattern of Bioluminescence. *Acts & Facts.* 42 (4): 18.

7. Gesenius, W. 1853. *Hebrew and Chaldee Lexicon to the Old Testament Scriptures.* S. P. Tregelles, trans. London: S. Bagster & Sons.

8. Some explorers continue to track evidence of living pterosaurs in very remote locations, and in particular Papua New Guinea's Umboi Island. Living pterosaurs would confirm biblical creation.

9. Avigad, N. 1981. The Priest of Dor. In *Israel Inspiration Journal Reader, Vol. 2.* H. M. Orlinsky, ed. Jerusalem: Ktav Publishing House, 1: 1199.

10. Belon, P. 1553. *Les observations de plusieurs singularitez et choses memorables trouvées en Grèce, Asie, Judée, Egypte, Arabie et autres pays étrangèrsm.* Paris.

11. Here is an example from Wales, from possibly as late as the 19th century: "The woods around Penllyne Castle, Glamorgan, had the reputation of being frequented by winged serpents, and these were the terror of old and young alike. An aged inhabitant of Penllyne, who died a few years ago, said that in his boyhood the winged serpents were described as very beautiful. They were coiled when in repose, and 'looked as though they were covered with jewels of all sorts. Some of them had crests sparkling with all the colours of the rainbow.' When disturbed, they glided swiftly, 'sparkling all over,' to their hiding-places. When angry, they 'flew over people's heads, with outspread wings bright, and sometimes with eyes, too, like the feathers in a peacock's tail.' He said it was 'no old story,' invented to 'frighten children,' but real fact. His father and uncles had killed some of them, for they were 'as bad as foxes for poultry.' This old man attributed the extinction of winged serpents to the fact that they were 'terrors in the farmyards and coverts.'" From Trevelyan, M. 1973. *Folk-Lore and Folk-Stories of Wales.* Yorkshire, UK: EP Publishing Limited, 169, 170.

12. Flavius Josephus. 2006. *Jewish Antiquities.* London: Bibliophile Books. Chapter 10, segments 245-247: 76.

13. Esarhaddon, Fragment F, Vol. 1-19 (Borger 1956: 112-13); older translations are Luckenbill 1927, II: 220 ([section] 559) and Oppenheim 1969: 292-93.

14. Herodotus. *The History of Herodotus.* G. C. Macaulay, trans. EBook #2707, Release Date December 1, Last Updated: January 25, 2013.

15. It appears to this author that Jonah actually died in the *ketos*, then was resurrected before being deposited on land nearer Nineveh. After all, Jesus likened His prophesied journey into the heart of the Earth to Jonah, and Jonah said that he journeyed below the mountains before God brought him "out of the belly of hell" (Jonah 2). Only his soul could make this journey. If so, then it might be more accurate to say that the *ketos* held Jonah's *body* for three days, while his soul journeyed to hell (Hebrew *sheol*) and back.

16. Cooper, B. 2012. *The Authenticity of the Book of Jonah.* Amazon Digital Services, 22.

4

TWO QUESTIONS ABOUT
DINOSAURS AND THE BIBLE

The story that the "Age of Reptiles" ended 65 million years ago is so widely believed perhaps because most people have never heard the evidence against it.

When I speak on the subject of dinosaurs, my audiences often hear for the first time two lines of scientific evidence that confirm dinosaurs lived and died thousands, not millions, of years ago. They also hear that there are real scientists who believe Genesis means exactly what it says.

Two Lines of Evidence

An egg timer can help us understand and communicate the processes involved in these lines of evidence. We can only wind an egg timer back until the dial stops. If it's a one-hour timer, then the maximum time it can continuously tick—assuming a constant tick rate and that no outside forces move the dial—is about one hour.

Similarly, the maximum length of time that bone collagen can "tick" if held at 45 degrees Fahrenheit is about 900,000 years, according to repeatable experiments performed by secular researchers. After less than a million years, assuming reasonable Earth-surface temperatures, the collagen protein timer goes "ding," at which point virtually all the protein has irreversibly fizzled into tiny chemicals. So each time paleontologists describe collagen in dinosaur bone—and they've been reporting it since the 1960s—they reinforce the dilemma evolutionists have of trying to explain why the collagen egg timer is still "ticking" in dinosaurs that are supposedly millions of years old.

The second egg timer-like line of evidence is the radiocarbon that keeps turning up in dinosaurs, other fossils, and carbon-containing earth materials. *Radiocarbon* refers to radioactive carbon atoms. All living cells contain at least some radiocarbon. These rare atoms take several thousand years to release their stored energy. Archaeologists use the radiocarbon decay system to estimate ages of ancient organic artifacts, but secular paleontologists do not use it to assign dates to dinosaur fossils because they know that carbon dating only works reliably for artifacts that are thousands of years old. They think that trying to carbon-date a dinosaur would be a waste of time since dinosaurs died millions of years ago. But creation scientists are not shackled by a belief in millions of years, so we are open to looking for radiocarbon in fossils. My colleagues and I have accumulated over three dozen carbon dates for dinosaurs from various locations, and this adds to dozens of carbon dates published in science journals and magazines for fossils found alongside or beneath dinosaur remains. Also, secular journals have reported perhaps a hundred

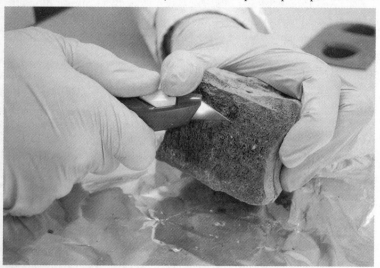

The author extracts bone material from the interior of a hadrosaur vertebra for carbon dating.
Image: Institute for Creation Research

carbon dates for ancient materials like coal, natural gas, shells, bone, and diamonds.

But the radiocarbon egg timer is even shorter than collagen's timer. It goes "ding" after only 100,000 years, after which point all the detectable radiocarbon should have spontaneously decayed into stable nitrogen.[1] So, every time we measure radiocarbon that comes from the fossil itself and not from a contaminant, we are confronted with solid scientific evidence that confirms these dinosaurs did not die millions or even hundreds of thousands of years ago, but only tens of thousands or fewer years ago.

While these results fit smoothly with the perspective that God created the whole cosmos about 6,000 years ago—in accordance with a straightforward reading of the chronological information found throughout Scripture—these same results generate tension for people who hold to an evolutionary "Age of Reptiles." Even many Christians shy away from a literal understanding of Genesis and try to accommodate evolution's billions of years. After learning that credentialed scientists believe God made dinosaurs on Day Six of the creation week and that Noah's Flood formed dinosaur fossils only thousands of years ago, my audiences often ask me two good questions. The first question deals with ways to merge billions of years with the Bible's timeline.

Question 1: Do Billions of Years Fit with Genesis?

Many Christians think that if they could somehow find room in the Scriptures for billions of years, then the conflict between Genesis and evolution is solved. They might not admit it, but sometimes they desire an easy way out so they don't have to investigate the sciences and the Scriptures involved. It can be taxing, but it can also be fascinating and very rewarding work. By sharing my own story, I hope to inspire brave new inquiries into deeply ingrained beliefs about the history of our world.

As a fully indoctrinated evolutionist, biology student, and follower of Christ, I experienced several phases in my journey to find the answer to the dinosaur time puzzle—which I later learned was more a question about whose word to trust regarding past events than about science or religion. I wanted answers, and I wanted the truth. Did dinosaurs really die out 65 million years ago, as I had been told almost since I could speak? If they did, what was I supposed to do with Genesis and its mere thousands of years? I can identify with those who look for ways to merge Scripture with millions of years because I tried it, too. In a nutshell, here is what I found.

"Days" in Genesis 1

I remember a conversation about origins with a friend. I was looking for answers, and he boldly told me his solution. He wagged his finger in emphasis as he quoted 2 Peter 3:8: "With the Lord one day is as a thousand years." He said this meant that each of the creation days took a thousand years, and thus who knows how many other literal days went unmentioned in the creation account? It sounded reasonable at first but easily crumbled under critique. What about the rest of the 2 Peter verse— "and a thousand years as one day"? Using my friend's logic, shouldn't this mean that a thousand years in Genesis only took one literal day?

Also, denying that creation days were ordinary 24-hour days makes mincemeat out of the Fourth Commandment (Exodus 20:8-10). The creation days form the very basis of our workweek that God Himself wrote onto Moses' stone tablets. I examined Genesis 1 again, finding that its author could not have been any more explicit in his definition of a day as the interval incorporating morning and evening, which merely needs a rotating Earth near a light source. The sun has served as that source since Day Four, and perhaps God's own glory served during the first three days.

Adding thousands of years to the Bible's account like my friend insisted on doing contributes a mere drop to the oceans of time that evolutionary thinking demands. It didn't take me long to realize that although a day is like a thousand years and a thousand years is like a day to God, who exists outside of time, the creation days were clearly defined as ordinary days in Genesis 1.

Squeezing the "Age of Dinosaurs" Between Verses

Next I considered the possibility of an eons-long time gap between Genesis 1:1 and 1:2, including the Age of Reptiles that I grew up believing. I held this view for quite a while. It allowed rocks to form at the evolutionary rates I expected and allowed dinosaurs to fossilize at the evolutionary times I learned from natural history museums, television documentaries, school textbooks, popular movies, and trusted friends. In this view, the Bible's timeline picks up where evolutionary time leaves off. But problems persistently dogged my theory of a giant time gap before Day One.

For example, in Genesis and later Scriptures that refer back to Genesis, why did the biblical authors so thoroughly avoid terms that even hint at the vast time that dominates evolutionary cosmic history? If Genesis 1 includes a massive time gap, then why did Jesus quote Genesis 1 as though it is real history in Mark 10:6—"But from the beginning of the creation, God 'made them male and female'"—instead of saying something like, "But billions of years after the Big Bang beginning, God 'made them male and female'"? If Genesis holds an enormous time gap, no author of Scripture seems to have heard about it. When Isaiah, Jeremiah, Jesus, and Paul presented creation, it was always according to the literal Genesis account.

The first verses of the Bible, as well as the entire first chapter of Genesis, sound like a plainly spoken narrative of step-by-step events, with no hint of a gap. We link events in narratives all the time. I could say, "I prepared for a day of work. I was hungry. I filled a bowl with cereal. I stayed in the kitchen until I finished breakfast." Did I *really* mean, "I prepared for a day of work. Then a million years passed. I was hungry. I filled a bowl with cereal"? After thinking through these possibilities, it became apparent to me that the motivations for inserting a gigantic time gap in Genesis always come from outside the Bible and not from any need within Scripture to do so. And if I couldn't trust Genesis and the Scriptures that refer to Genesis, what parts of the Bible could I trust?

Creation by Evolution?

I had also considered the idea that God used evolution to create all things—pulsars, planets, protozoa, pine trees, *Parasaurolophus*, and people—over billions of years. If we ignore the "days" defined by "morning and evening" in Genesis 1, maybe the creation account actually mirrors a long evolutionary history. Perhaps God created dinosaurs not on a literal Day Six but long after He allowed stars and trees to evolve, and millions of years before Adam and Eve arrived.

It shouldn't take long for an honest inquiry to clearly show that evolution and Genesis cannot be spliced together without making liberal use of large, sharp scissors to slice and dice the creation account. Some of the same arguments used above apply just as much to this merger attempt. For example, discounting the literal days of creation erases the basis for our six workday and one rest-day week as specified in the Ten Commandments. And if we jettison the basis for one of those commandments, then the door cracks open to eject them all.

I finally had enough of the Genesis compromises when I learned that they all undermine the works of Christ on the cross—works that had set me free from sin and selfishness when I repented of my wrongs and trusted Christ as my Savior. These compromises all mean that dinosaurs and other animals died and became fossils long before Adam's sin. But according to Scripture, death invaded the world as a result of sin (Romans 5:12). The whole reason the Lord Jesus died was to pay our sin-earned death penalty—a penalty that marred every aspect of a once "very good" creation where even dinosaurs ate vegetable matter and not animal flesh.[2] The Genesis compromises erase the reason for Jesus' ministry and sacrifice.

Fortunately, good science does not demand that we squeeze billions of years into the creation account, nor does it force us to doubt the Bible and the very character of God. The collagen and radiocarbon lines of scientific evidence give us confidence that God got His history exactly right after all. But this leads to a second important question.

Question 2: How Could Most Scientists Be Wrong?

After I share the two scientific evidences for recent dinosaur deposition—the collagen and the radiocarbon timers—the second question my audiences ask deals with the authority of scientists. Either the Word of God Almighty is dead wrong about a thousands-of-years-old cosmos, or secular scientists are dead wrong about millions of years. The evidence in this small book demonstrates that people—not God—are at fault. But how could so many scientists be so wrong about when dinosaurs lived and died?

First, scientists don't exactly have a clean record for accuracy, even on major points. A few centuries ago they scoffed at germ theory, which eventually became the basis for successful medical practices. The prevailing opinion among scientists once held that only four elements—earth, air, fire, and water—comprise all materials. Rigorous experiments performed by those willing to challenge this doctrine revealed scores of unique atoms now familiarly organized in the periodic table of elements. Scientific majorities have been wrong in the past, and since scientists are fallible people, they can still be wrong.

For example, many secular scientists accept the idea that inanimate chemicals evolved into the first living cell. But because each cell contains libraries of coded specifications like blueprints for building what the cell needs, this is like claiming that natural processes brought plastic, glass, and metal together to form the first personal computer. What motivates secularists to adhere to such an improbable scenario? Whatever the cause, this life-by-accident idea finds no affirmations from lab bench experiments.

How Secularism Works

At its core, secular thinking rejects miracles. Its adherents discard the notion of God working uniquely in space and time. Was Jesus conceived by God's Holy Spirit? Without even examining the relevant history, secularists say no. Did the Flood cover the entire sphere of Earth? Impossible, say secularists, who "cannot allow a divine foot in the door," to quote scientist Richard Lewontin from his favorable review of an atheist book.[3] Secularism's anti-Bible bias leads to suggestions that Noah's Flood only covered certain regions, like the Black Sea or the Fertile Crescent. Without the possibility of miracles, God is taken out of science, origins, and out of a secularist's life. So when it comes to dinosaurs, secular thinking has no place, or patience, for the literal days of creation.

Most scientists see the world through secular eyes, perhaps inheriting this perspective from their parents and/or professors. Scientific culture may affirm secularism even more strongly than the broader culture does, for example, by funding and publishing predominantly studies that strictly present evolutionary history. Once beliefs form and settle within our minds, they become difficult to dislodge. Several times in discussions after my presentations, secularists have told me that even though the evidence from collagen and carbon appears to support a recent origin for dinosaur fossils, they trust that scientists will someday discover why collagen and radiocarbon have been able to last millions of years. Isn't that just blind faith?

Jesus faced this difficult aspect of fallen human nature when He dealt with the Pharisees. Jesus showed them all the evidence needed to prove He was God, yet the Pharisees understood none of it. He lived without sin, taught the truth, told the future, and performed miracle after miracle right in front of them. Once, after He had stilled wind and waves, healed many who were sick, and cast demons out of some who were possessed, "the Pharisees said, 'He casts out demons by the ruler of the demons'" (Matthew 9:34). How ridiculous. And the Pharisees were the most learned men in that culture. Perhaps not much has changed after all this time.

Dating Dinosaur Fossils

Could a secular bias influence the process of assigning ages to dinosaur fossils? When secularists assign dates to dinosaur fossils, they often

Dinosaurs died millions of years ago.

Dinosaur fossils are millions of years old.

Dating dinosaur fossils by circular reasoning. Images: Bigstock

do so with painstaking care. I have read many technical reports, and they include tedious details of rock types, surveys of fossils (including pollen grains) found among dinosaurs, as well as references to other workers' related results. When I suggest that they consistently reach some wrong answers, I am not accusing them of carelessness. But by bringing in the belief that dinosaurs lived and died millions of years ago, is it possible that this same scientific carefulness can be used to override evidence that contradicts evolution's timeline?

To see how biases might steer their thinking, consider how secular scientists have dealt with out-of-place fossils. Sometimes, dinosaur remains occur in rock layers designated as *younger* than 65 million years. This does not fit the dogma that all dinosaurs had died by then. How does the secular mind-set deal with these discoveries? At least three options come into play:

1. Admit that some dinosaurs survived the supposed 65-million-year extinction event.

2. Assign new ages to the troublesome dinosaur-containing rock layers.

3. Invent a story that explains away the evidence. For example, claim that dinosaur remains from older layers were dislodged and redeposited in the younger layer, or that the remains aren't from dinosaurs after all.

Which options do secularists most often choose? Retired meteorologist and creation researcher Michael Oard helpfully summarized some examples.[4] In 2012, scientists reported three-toed tracks in rocks from Washington state. Other researchers had used various methods to support their belief that the rocks were deposited long *after* the end of their Mesozoic Age of Reptiles. Since the authors of the 2012 study were confident that dinosaurs had all died before these Washington rocks formed, they asserted that an extinct giant flightless bird made the tracks. Only a handful of giant bird tracks have been discovered, but billions of dinosaur tracks occur worldwide. The scientists wrote that had they found these same tracks in rock layers designated as Mesozoic, they would have immediately identified them as three-toed dinosaur tracks. In this case, secular convictions about rock ages—not an objective study of bird and dinosaur foot structure—directed their fossil identification.

Bible-believing scientists have a bias, too, and it opens new options to explain dinosaur fossils and rocks. The thickness and extent of rock layers like those with the three-toed tracks suggest that they formed from an unimaginably catastrophic water event consistent with the forces required for Noah's Flood to deluge the whole Earth, as Genesis clearly teaches. During the yearlong Flood, water may have laid down one sediment layer above another layer within months or even just days, not millions of years. From this perspective, identifying the tracks depends more on foot structure than on trying to make them fit the times the rock layers are supposed to represent.

In another example given by Michael Oard, secular scientists found a modern-looking monkey fossil in "dinosaur era" Mesozoic rocks in Chile. How did secularists explain this out-of-place fossil? They could have gone against evolutionary dogma by suggesting that modern monkeys—supposedly very recent products of evolution—actually lived long ago with dinosaurs. Instead, they erased 50 million years from the rock's original age assignment to fit their conviction that monkey fossils only occur in Cenozoic strata because those rocks represent a time when the monkeys supposedly lived.

Brian Thomas at Picket Wire Canyon next to a duck-billed dinosaur track. Images: Brian Thomas

Oard also described an age reassignment in the Picket Wire Canyonlands, located in Colorado north of Amarillo. In the summer of 2014, I endured a blazing hot mid-August investigation of this arid canyon. One of the world's highest concentrations of sauropod dinosaur tracks drew me to the limestone layers in the canyon's floor, which is only reachable by biking or hiking six miles.

Since these sauropods lived during Jurassic times, according to evolutionary history, secular scientists were originally confident the rocks should be designated as Jurassic. But the discovery of Triassic fossils found *above* these supposedly Jurassic dinosaur tracks complicated that decision. The fossils were in the wrong evolutionary order. How was this handled? The scientists "solved" the problem by declaring the Jurassic rocks were now Triassic.

Consider the reasoning involved in the researchers' conclusion: "Because the eolianite [supposedly wind-deposited rock layer] in the Picket Wire Canyonlands is overlain by deposits bearing *in situ* [buried when the rocks formed] fossils of late Triassic age, it cannot be the Middle Jurassic Entrada Sandstone, as it was identified by some previous authors."[5] Clearly, the secular notions that each rock layer represents an age separated from other layers by millions of years and that certain creatures lived in each age prompted this rock-reassignment maneuver. In a rare moment of clarity, one secular scientist wrote:

> Geologists themselves must take much of the responsibility for the dissemination of this concept [of sudden, worldwide dinosaur extinction] because they have often defined the end of the Age of Reptiles or Mesozoic Era as the exact time that dinosaurs became extinct. Ergo, reasoning in a tight circle, dinosaurs became extinct at the end of the Mesozoic time.[6]

In other words, secular thinking does not necessarily derive millions of years *from* rocks or fossils, but it certainly imposes vast lengths of time *on* rocks and fossils. How could so many scientists be wrong about dinosaur ages? Sometimes it is because belief in evolutionary history plays a larger role than evidence when making dinosaur age assignments.

The Lord Jesus also faced strong bias. John wrote:

> Then the Jews took up stones again to stone Him. Jesus answered them, "Many good works I have shown you from My Father. For which of those works do you stone Me?" The Jews answered Him, saying, "For a good work we do not stone You, but for blasphemy, and because You, being a Man, make Yourself God" (John 10:31-33).

These religious Jews reasoned that although Jesus claimed to be God, as a mere man He could not be God and thus should suffer the death penalty for blasphemy. Their bias against the possibility of God coming to Earth as a man—not the evidence for or against Jesus being God—steered them toward rejecting His divinity. Similarly, secularists' bias against dinosaurs being created according to the Genesis account—not the evidence for or against millions of years—may steer them toward rejecting a thousands-of-years Earth history.

What About Radioisotope "Clocks"?

So far, we have examined the question of whether secular scientists are wrong about the timing of dinosaurs by considering how circular reasoning and evolutionary assumptions—not science—drive their age assignments. Secularists claim that radioisotope "ages" objectively and scientifically confirm rocks' millions-of-years history, but this claim crumbles under scrutiny.

Radioisotopes are varieties of atoms (isotopes) that emit radiation and particles, eventually decaying into stable, nonradioactive atoms. Age estimates are based on measuring the amounts of radioactive versus stable atoms in a rock. Secularists select the slower-decaying radioisotope systems to estimate ages for crystalline rocks like granite and basalt. Secular scientists often assign ages to dinosaur-containing rocks by using radioisotope age assignments given to ancient lava flows found above or beneath them. But in order to convert measurements of radioactive versus stable atoms into ages, one must assume a constant history for these crystalline rocks.

How accurate is such an assumption? First, consider radioisotope ages assigned to rocks of known age. Here are some examples that secular scientists have published:[7]

Location	Known Age	Isotope Age
Mt. Erebus	17 yrs	1.6 my
Mt. Etna basalt	29 yrs	35 my
Mt. Etna basalt	37 yrs	0.7 my
Mt. Stromboli	38 yrs	2.4 my
Kilauea Iki	40 yrs	8.5 my
Mt. Lassen plagioclase	85 yrs	11 my
Kilauea basalt	<200 yrs	21 my
Hualalai basalt	200 yrs	0.6 my
Sunset Crater basalt	950 yrs	27 my
Mt. Etna basalt	2,100 yrs	25 my

my = millions of years   © Institute for Creation Research

Creation researchers have made similar finds. For example, in 1996 Dr. Steve Austin described radioisotope results from crystalline rock collected at Mount St. Helens. Witnesses saw the lava harden to rock in 1986, six years after the famous 1980 eruption. The secular lab reported rock "ages" of about 0.35, 0.34, and 2.8 million years.[8] Two million years for a ten-year-old rock? Something's very wrong here.

Years of diligent and fruitful research sponsored in large part by the Institute for Creation Research have identified core problems with each major radioisotope system used to date rocks. It turns out that the flaws in radioisotope dating do not arise from inaccurate isotope counts but from overconfidence in the accuracy of the assumptions needed to convert those counts into "ages."

For example, the isotope system used for the Mount St. Helens samples showed inflated ages because the lava from which the rock hardened contained extra amounts of stable versus radioactive atoms. In this case, the melting process did not reset the radioisotope "clock" to zero, as the secular dating method requires. In another major discovery, three lines of evidence showed that the decay of uranium to lead occurred billions of times faster in the past than it does today.[9] Thus, "ages" from the uranium-lead radioisotope system cannot be trusted either. Dozens of relevant articles at icr.org document these issues with technical details, but suffice it to say that radioisotope clocks are worse than broken wall clocks that at least get the time right twice a day. Meanwhile, in a further example of secular circular reasoning, faulty radioisotope results are selected to supply "dates" that fit secular age expectations.

Physicist Jake Hebert has brought together specific examples of circularity in dating methods such as radioisotope dating. He showed how an array of methods like radioisotopes, seafloor sediments, astronomical cycles, ice cores, and magnetic seafloor signatures all inform and influence one another, and they all tie back to evolutionary expectations. Secularists sometimes boast that each method independently verifies deep time, but Dr. Hebert has dug up the details from secular science literature showing the ways in which one biased technique influences, tunes, dates, filters, or calibrates other methods.[10] If it were truly scientific, each method would stand on its own, with no need of external "calibration." And if such methods were scientific, we would not discover the evolutionary assumption of millions of years embedded in each one—but we do. By these complicated machinations, secularists ensure that rocks and fossils

Faith in Millions of Years
↓
Astronomical Theory
↓
Radioisotope "Ages"
↓
Faith in Millions of Years

Secular scientists use the assumption of millions of years to calibrate their dating methods to achieve the expected results, which are then used to justify their millions-of-years belief.

receive the age assignments they expect, and they insulate these expectations behind thick and convoluted layers of technical jargon and webs of cross-referencing.

In answer to our first question about Genesis and billions of years, we found no way to squeeze evolutionary history into the Bible without damaging God's Word and even the gospel. And the evidences of collagen and radiocarbon decay confirm Scripture's history of thousands, not millions, of years. In answer to the second question, we have found that a secular bias against the supernatural working of God in creation helps explain how so many scientists could be wrong about dinosaur ages. Bias can even steer our thinking in a certain direction despite evidence to the contrary, like the Pharisees' failure to identify Jesus as God. One last aspect of the secular mind-set should complete our answer to the second question about how so many scientists could be wrong about dinosaur history—namely, that the force that drives some to secularism and its circular reasoning has its root in the spiritual realm.

A Spiritual Cause and Cure

What kind of evidence would we expect to find if dinosaurs, sea serpents, and pterosaurs lived alongside man in recent human history? What else could we expect except exactly what history so abundantly provides—eyewitness written accounts, carvings, and paintings? The ancient world is stacked with evidence that strongly supports the idea that Scripture refers directly to dinosaurs (behemoth), marine reptiles (leviathan and *ketos*), and pterosaurs (*nachash saraph*).

This contrasts with evolutionary history, which asserts that such creatures died millions of years before man "evolved." Clearly, those who make that assertion must carefully avoid anatomy, archaeology, history, and the Bible. It is just such people that the apostle Peter had in mind when he urged the church in the last days to be wary of "scoffers" (2 Peter 3:3) who would slickly insert their false, antibiblical teachings "among the people" in the church (2 Peter 2:1).

Peter told us exactly what these dangerous scoffers would believe about the past: They would "willingly forget" (i.e., deliberately ignore) the two most widely evident miracles of all time—the creation of the world when God commanded the heavens and Earth to stand out of the water, and the judgment of the world when it was destroyed by that water (2 Peter 3:5-6). In other words, Peter foretold that people would introduce false teachings to generate disbelief in the Genesis creation and the Genesis Flood. These are the same two biblical events that evolutionists most often mock today.

Denying the historical realities of creation and the Flood is shameful for Christians because these realities undergird our most basic knowledge of who God is. The creation displays God's power, and the Flood signifies His right to judge sin. This basic knowledge of history is necessary to fully comprehend the gospel, and it grounds our understanding of dinosaurs. The Genesis creation best explains dinosaur origins by design, and the Genesis Flood best explains dinosaur fossils. And the Bible's clear references to humans and dinosaurs living at the same time best explain the numerous records of flying, swimming, and walking extinct reptiles to which world history attests.

Why do secular scoffers work so hard to avoid history and God's Word? Often it is because they wish to ignore a god with the power and holiness to judge sin. Their active ignorance compels them to rewrite history into a form in which man is responsible only to himself. Their man-made alternate version of the past is what masquerades today as "science" and needlessly robs many Christians of their confidence in God's Word. Fortunately, the Bible contains flawless history of the early Earth. All who read it can understand exactly where we came from, where sin and corruption came from, and why we need a Savior to rescue us from certain judgment.

Peter wrote that the scoffers would mock the coming judgment, saying, "Where is the promise of His coming?" (2 Peter 3:4). In contrast to the words of sin-blinded men who mindlessly dismiss the events recorded in Scripture and described by the ancients, we can wholeheartedly trust the words of our faithful and true Creator of dinosaurs, humans, and everything else this universe contains. For certainly, "the day of the Lord will come" (2 Peter 3:10).

Have you prepared yourself by trusting Christ as your Savior, seeking Him, and obeying God's principles and promises? He stands ready to receive and redeem each of us, for "God so loved the world that He gave His only begotten Son, that whoever believes in Him should not perish but have everlasting life" (John 3:16).

Notes

1. Again, this assumes that the nuclei of radioactive carbon atoms would have been decaying at the same rate the whole time, and it assumes that no person or process added or subtracted radiocarbon to or from the sample.
2. Genesis 1:30.
3. Lewontin, R. Billions and Billions of Demons. *The New York Review of Books.* Posted on nybooks.com January 9, 1997.
4. Oard, M. 2013. The reinforcement syndrome ubiquitous in the earth sciences. *Journal of Creation.* 27 (3): 13-16.
5. Heckert, A. B. et al. 2012. Triassic fossils found stratigraphically above "Jurassic" eolianites necessitate the revision of lower Mesozoic stratigraphy in Picket Wire Canyonlands, south-central Colorado. *Rocky Mountain Geology.* 47 (1): 37–53.
6. Jepsen, G. L. 1964. Riddles of the terrible lizards. *American Scientist.* 52 (2): 236.
7. See references in Snelling, A. A. 1999. "Excess Argon": The "Archilles' Heel" of Potassium-Argon and Argon-Argon "Dating" of Volcanic Rocks. *Acts & Facts.* 28 (1).
8. Austin, S. A. 1996. Excess Argon within Mineral Concentrates from the New Dacite Lava Dome at Mount St. Helens Volcano. *Creation Ex Nihilo Technical Journal.* 10 (3): 335–343.
9. Vardiman, L., A. A. Snelling, and E. F. Chaffin, eds. 2005. *Radioisotopes and the Age of the Earth: Results of a Young-Earth Creationist Research Initiative.* El Cajon, CA: Institute for Creation Research and Chino Valley, AZ: Creation Research Society.
10. Hebert, J. 2014. Circular Reasoning in the Dating of Deep Seafloor Sediments and Ice Cores: The Orbital Tuning Method. *Answers Research Journal.* 7: 297–309.

ABOUT THE AUTHOR

Brian Thomas received his bachelor's degree in biology in 1993 and a master's in biotechnology in 1999 from Stephen F. Austin State University, Nacogdoches, Texas. He taught junior high and high school at Christian schools in Texas, as well as biology, chemistry, and anatomy as an adjunct and assistant professor at Dallas area universities. Since 2008 Mr. Thomas has been the Science Writer at ICR, where he contributes news and magazine articles, speaks on creation issues, and researches original tissue fossils. He is a contributor to *Guide to Creation Basics, Creation Basics & Beyond,* and *Guide to Dinosaurs.*

Guide to Dinosaurs
Institute for Creation Research

Dinosaurs were amazing creatures. From the time the first dinosaur bones were unearthed, the story of these unusual beasts has captivated people of all ages. We are learning a lot about them from the fossil record, but there are still many questions:

- When, where, and how did dinosaurs live?
- How did they go extinct?
- What does the fossil evidence tell us about them?

Explore the fascinating history of these animals, the many different kinds that existed, and the discoveries made by dinosaur hunters and paleontologists.

Guide to God's Animals
Frank Sherwin

How do fish breathe and birds fly? Why do some animals migrate and others hibernate? And what happened to the dinosaurs and other extinct animals?

The animal kingdom is a massive and amazing part of God's wonderful creation, with creatures that fly, swim, slither, gallop, swing through trees, and much more. Discover the fascinating details of what makes each animal unique and how they are engineered to live in their own habitat.

ABOUT THE
INSTITUTE FOR CREATION RESEARCH

Founded by Dr. Henry Morris in 1970, ICR exists to conduct scientific research within the realms of origins and Earth history and to educate through training programs, conferences, media presentations, and print resources. ICR was established for three main purposes:

Research: ICR conducts laboratory, field, theoretical, and library research on projects that seek to understand the science of origins and Earth history. ICR scientists have conducted numerous research projects in various locations and on vital issues such as Radioisotopes and the Age of the Earth (RATE), Flood-Activated Sedimentation and Tectonics (FAST), the human genome, and other topics related to geology, genetics, and much more.

Education: ICR offers courses and seminars that train men and women to do real-world apologetics with a foundation of biblical authority and creation science. ICR also offers a one-year, nondegree training program called the Creationist Worldview.

Communication: ICR produces books, videos, periodicals, and other media to communicate its research findings and related information. ICR's main publication is *Acts & Facts*, a free full-color magazine with a readership of more than 250,000, and the website www.icr.org features regular and relevant creation science updates.

For more information, go to
www.icr.org